The
Comprehensive
Guide to
Social Security and
Medicare

By

Ken Stern

The
Comprehensive
Guide to
Social Security and
Medicare

By

Ken Stern

CAREER PRESS
180 Fifth Avenue
P.O. Box 34
Hawthorne, NJ 07507
1-800-CAREER-1
201-427-0229 (outside U.S.)
FAX: 201-427-2037

THE COMPREHENSIVE GUIDE TO SOCIAL SECURITY AND MEDICARE
ISBN 1-56414-172-1, $11.99
Cover design by The Visual Group
Printed in the U.S.A. by Book-mart Press

To order this title by mail, please include price as noted above, $2.50 handling per order, and $1.00 for each book ordered. Send to: Career Press, Inc., 180 Fifth Ave., P.O. Box 34, Hawthorne, NJ 07507

Or call toll-free 1-800-CAREER-1 (Canada: 201-427-0229) to order using VISA or MasterCard, or for further information on books from Career Press.

Library of Congress Cataloging-in-Publication Data

Stern, Ken, 1965-
    The comprehensive guide to social security and medicare / by Ken Stern.
        p.   cm.
    Includes index.
    ISBN 1-56414-172-1 : $11.99
    1. Social security--United States. 2. Medicare. I. Title.
HD7125.S734   1995
368.4'3'00973--dc20   94-46690
                                                                          CIP

Acknowledgments

To my wonderful supportive staff, especially James O'Brien and Evie Ruiz, whose research savvy helped immeasurably. My publisher, Ron Fry of Career Press, for his belief in me. Bob Newman, for introducing me to the publisher and also for his skill as a publicist. Most importantly, I want to thank my radio listeners and the readers of my *Mature American* newsletter. Your support, your questions and your continued desire to learn served as my inspiration for this book.

Contents

Introduction

Truth

As a *working person* you receive a paycheck. Last Friday, when you received your paycheck, you probably glanced at it. You checked the hours you worked to make sure they were accurate. However, you glossed over the biggest deduction, "FICA," and the other taxes because you don't understand those deductions and assumed they were for the government. You are not alone. Very few workers ever check their Social Security earnings even though this is a huge deduction. Why should you check your earnings? Why will it help to know where this money goes? Read on.

Truth

As an *employer* it seems as though the tax you pay for Social Security and Medicare just keeps going up. You pay this tax for every employee. Are there ways to reduce this tax? If you could reduce this tax, would it leave more money in your pocket? You bet it would.

Truth

You are 67 years of age and you retired several years ago. Now you feel that a little extra income, along with something more to do during the day, would enhance your retirement. However, after figuring out how much your job would pay and how much your Social Security benefits would be reduced, you find out that you would almost be working for free. Are there any ways you can work without diminishing your Social Security payments substantially?

Truth

Like many retirees, you are proud of all that you have contributed to the country in taxes and Social Security. However, now you want to enjoy the benefits to which you are entitled. But, it seems unfair that your Social Security benefits are being taxed so heavily. Can you reduce the taxes you pay on your Social Security benefits?

Truth

When you retired you looked forward to enjoying "the golden years." You thought that you had saved enough money to live comfortably. However, you did not allocate any money for medical costs because you thought Medicare would take care of these expenses. Unfortunately, you now learn that Medicare pays very little of these expenses. You're now stuck with the burden of higher medical costs that are likely to severely affect your retirement. What can you do about this?

Truth

More than 135 million workers contributed to Social Security, Medicare, disability and related entitlement programs through payroll taxes last year. Some 43 million individuals will receive monthly benefits this year. Entitlement programs are the largest Federal budget item. Needless to say, this issue should be of concern to you. Not only do you need to understand the system to make sure that you receive all you are entitled to receive, but you should also understand the system to make certain you don't allow our elected officials to take away what we have worked and paid so much for.

People are always trying to "optimize" their efforts. Don't you deserve the highest salary for your efforts? When you invest, you want the best return for the least amount of risk. So why don't you pay attention to the benefits you're entitled to? How many of you check the amount you receive from Social Security to verify its accuracy? Do you assume the Social Security Administration is infallible and never makes a mistake? How many of you have appealed a decision when you were denied Medicare? There are more than seven million survivors receiving survivor's benefits but there may be countless more who are unaware that they are entitled to benefits.

The entitlement programs include Social Security, Medicare, Medicaid and other programs associated with these organizations. The amount of money you will spend to maintain these programs over your lifetime is incredible. No doubt, many of us will contribute far more than we will receive back in benefits. Furthermore, our lawmakers are constantly looking for ways to reduce Social Security benefits but still impose higher taxes for these reduced benefits. Medicare used to cover the majority of medical costs incurred by retirees. Now, because of deductibles and medical needs that are not covered by Medicare, Medicare will most likely cover less than 40 percent of the medical expenses you'll have when you're retired.

Even worse news, as some of you may have already realized, is that your largest medical expenses are for illnesses not covered by Medicare at all! The position of Congress has been made clear: To receive any aid for services not covered, you must be broke. If you're not poverty stricken, then your property can be liened after your death.

The bottom line: We are living longer, but at a higher cost than ever before. Many of us will suffer a disability, illness or die and our families will desperately need Social Security benefits. Sadly, because so many people don't understand the complex system, many of these deserving people won't receive the benefits to which they are entitled. As a result, you will spend too much of your own money, not receive the type or quality of care you deserve and, ultimately, you may die poverty stricken as a result of the inadequacies and intricacies of our system.

So many programs have been set up to help seniors. Benefits range from help in paying bills, meal service, hospice care and disability benefits. However, because they don't know what is available, they end up paying more.

Don't allow this to happen to you. Educate yourself. This book provides a broad overview of the Social Security system. Once you know your specific needs, you can get help. Use the agencies, hotlines and local professional help (many sources are provided in this text) to insure you receive all the assistance that you deserve.

As baby-boomers become eligible for many of these benefits, these "entitlement programs" will become the subject of heated debates. Politicians will be talking about the future of the benefits. You *must* know where you stand on these issues so you'll know how to vote for *your* future.

Chapter 1

Introduction and overview of Social Security

Origin of Social Security

If people are afraid to retire without any guaranteed income today, imagine how they felt before the Social Security Act was passed. One of the greatest fears of citizens, especially during the Great Depression years, was that they could never afford to retire. To address this concern, Congress passed the Social Security Act which President Franklin D. Roosevelt signed into law on August 14, 1935.

The Social Security Act was designed to meet several needs. The Act created the Old Age Survivors' and Disability Insurance Program (OASDI). Its primary goal was to provide economic security for "covered" workers and their families by providing some level of income after the worker retired, died or became disabled. This program is what are known today as retirement benefits.

Over the years, the Social Security Act has been amended to include:

1939 - Insurance for dependents and survivors

1951 - Insurance for the self-employed

1956 - Disability insurance

1965 - Medicare (health insurance for the elderly)

1974 - Supplemental Security Income (SSI) program

To administer Social Security, the Social Security Administration (SSA) was created. The SSA administers the Retirement, Survivors and Disability programs.

The Health Care Financing Administration (HCFA) is the federal agency that manages the Medicare, Medicaid and Hospice programs. Both of these organizations operate under the direction of the Department of Health and Human Services (HHS) which aids in administering the system.

However, in 1994, after years of discussion, the Senate approved splitting SSA from HHS, thus making the SSA an independent agency. Social Security now operates independently and is removed from many of the budget debates that focus on cuts in the department of Health and Human Services. There are still some people who want further cuts in the national budget and think these cuts should come from the entitlement programs.

There are really two types of entitlements. Social Security and Medicare are considered self-supporting because taxes go directly into trust funds set up for these organizations. Then, there are the entitlement programs that do cost Americans a great deal of money, and probably represent the largest single federal budget item. Among these programs are Medicaid, food stamps, housing assistance, etc.

Also know that many states have their own rules and regulations regarding coverage and benefits. If you have a specific problem, contact the Social Security office in your county or a local expert (The appendix lists in-state organizations).

Purpose of Social Security related programs

How much am I going to get? What do I need to do in order to get it? How much will it cost? What if I can't get it? This book will answer all of these important questions.

This text will explain the many exceptions and the ways to maximize your entitlements. These benefits are called entitlements because you are *entitled* to these benefits and more. Your primary concerns should be to find out what benefits you have coming to you and what these benefits will cost. The vast majority of people don't understand the system and as a result don't receive their fair share.

As defined, the Social Security Act (including subsequent amendments) has several purposes and programs. All of the services fall into five main categories. All of these categories will be defined and explained in other chapters but the following is a list of the five categories, along with simple definitions so that you can begin to understand this complex system.

Retirement income

This is a benefit offered to eligible retirees at age 65 or at age 62 for early retirement. This income was designed to supplement private pensions. Many retirees have come to rely on this benefit far too often.

Disability insurance

This program provides for benefits to you or a family member if you or a family member becomes disabled. This coverage was intended to replace some of the earnings that would be lost if you suffered a disability. However, the Social Security definition of disability is very stringent (see applicable section) and you should be prepared to meet these requirements if you apply for disability benefits.

Survivors' benefits

This program provides benefits for family members if an eligible worker dies. Even if a worker is not fully insured, survivors may still be able to receive benefits.

Health insurance benefits (Medicare & Medicaid)

This program was designed to provide health care coverage (primarily hospital coverage) to every eligible worker at age 65. Regardless of age, people who need medical care but do not have a sufficient amount of assets or income may still qualify for Medicaid.

Supplemental Security Income (SSI)

This program specifically provides a minimum income for needy individuals whether or not they are eligible for Social Security benefits.

In addition, many other benefits exist although they will not be discussed in detail in this book. You should be aware of these programs which include food stamps, Meals on Wheels and other special interest programs.

Applying for a Social Security number & card

Everyone should have a Social Security number and should also keep their Social Security card handy. If you have a child, you should notify Social Security after his or her birth and request a card for the baby. (You will need to include your child's Social Security number on your tax return.) If you are applying for United States citizenship, you will also receive a Social Security number. Most employers, banks, schools, etc. will need your Social Security number. If for some reason you don't have one, there are many ways you can easily get one.

Simply go to your local Social Security office or call 1-800-772-1213 and ask for the form necessary to receive a number. (You can even fill out the provided form located in the appendix.) Your phone book lists the local Social Security offices. If you are unable to leave your home or haven't any transportation, some offices will send a representative to your home.

If you lose your card, change names, divorce or remarry

If your name has changed, you should apply for a new card. Fill out the form and submit it to a Social Security office. Along with the form, you will need other identification such as a certified birth certificate, driver's license, marriage certificate or, if applicable, divorce papers.

When else to contact Social Security?

Whenever you have a major change in your life, you should notify Social Security by calling your local Social Security office or the national toll-free number (1-800-772-1213).

You should contact Social Security if your spouse or another close relative has died, if you're going back to work after being on disability or if you're changing your name because of a marriage or a divorce.

Where your Social Security taxes go

About 73 cents goes to a Social Security trust fund that pays monthly benefits to retirees, widows and widowers and children of deceased workers.

Nineteen cents goes to a Medicare trust fund to pay for Medicare beneficiaries.

Eight cents goes to a trust fund that pays benefits to people with disabilities.

(Information obtained through the SSA, 1994)

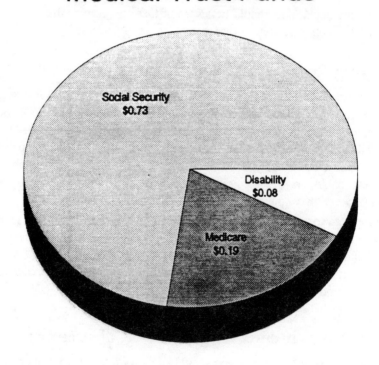

Medical Trust Funds

Summary

Social Security and Medicare offer a range of programs intended to assist recipients with a variety of needs. The five broad categories of this assistance are retirement income, disability benefits, survivors' benefits, health insurance and supplemental income programs. Because of the complexity of the system, it's important you learn the basics of the programs so that you can find out what benefits you may be eligible for. By doing some homework to understand the intricacies of the system, you will be able to take advantage of useful programs, some of which you never knew existed.

Chapter 2

Paying for Social Security

It isn't cheap! You will pay more for Social Security than for many other fixed expenses such as rent and utilities. Worse still, some people will never receive in benefits what they have contributed. If you have contributed $100,000 into Social Security over the last 20 years, retire and then pass away, your survivors' benefits will most likely not come close to that $100,000. Although some of you will receive more than you have contributed, Social Security is usually a poor investment.

All the benefits and programs of Social Security are financed by taxes on employers and employees. Almost everyone who owns a business or works for someone who owns a business will contribute into three trust funds: retirement, disability and health insurance.

As an employee, the amount you contribute and the handling of that contribution is regulated by the Federal Insurance Contributions Act (FICA). You may recall seeing a "FICA" deduction on your payroll check. If you are an employer, you contribute through the Self Employment Contributions Act (SECA).

The amount of money you will pay into Social Security is a percentage of your income and therefore changes every year. You should find out the new amount every year. As of 1995, these were the tax rates:

1995 taxes on earnings for Social Security

Employee (FICA)

Social Security   6.2 percent of earnings to $61,200

Medicare   1.45 percent of *all* earnings

The total rate is 7.65 percent up to $60,600 of earned income, then 1.45 percent on all further earnings.

SECA

Social Security   12.4 percent of earnings to $60,600

Medicare   2.9 percent of *all* earnings

Total rate of 15.3 percent to $61,200, then 2.9 percent on all further earnings.

The employee tax

The tax is expensive now but many elected officials want to raise it again. That's why it's important that you and your family are aware of all the benefits you are entitled to receive. Think of Social Security as a form of insurance; there are different ways the insurance will pay off. If you don't know what the payoffs are, there is a strong chance you will not receive all the benefits.

The employer tax

Employers pay a tax based on net earnings. The IRS definition says net earnings is net income after all expenses from a trade or distributive share of a partnership, such as dividends, capital gains, rental real estate, retirement payments, etc.

In the above chart, you see that an employer can be subject to tax on 15.3 percent of net earnings. This tax is calculated using a few simple rules:

Of all net earnings from self-employment, 92.35 percent is used. (This change took effect in 1990.) If your net earnings are less than $400, you don't pay any Social Security Tax.

As illustrated in the chart, the maximum amount Social Security can tax your pay changes every year (currently, in 1995, the maximum is $61,200). However, there is no maximum for the Medicare Hospital Insurance Tax, so you could be taxed on an unlimited amount of income with regard to this portion.

How employers can reduce the amount of Social Security tax imposed on the self-employed

Paying such a sizable percentage of your earnings into Social Security is undoubtedly a burden. Therefore, you should look at minimizing these costs. Remember, you pay the tax on "net earnings," as defined above. For Social Security purposes, net earnings are simply gross earnings from the business minus all allowable business deductions and depreciations.

As an employer, your net earnings from self-employment are reduced by an amount equal to half of your total self-employment tax. Secondly, half of your contributions into SECA are deductible as business expenses. However, the fact that you will be taxed continuously for every dollar you earn is very depressing.

This "unlimited tax" is relatively new; many self-employed individuals are still in shock. Here are some suggestions to reduce your Social Security liability:

1. Create an S Corporation and pay yourself as an employee. This strategy is most appropriate if you make between $75,000 to $100,000. You should check with your lawyer and accountant if you're considering setting up this type of corporation.

   The idea behind an S Corporation is that you're paid a salary as if you were an employee. Therefore, you would be taxed at the lower FICA rates and have a lower Social Security tax. Your Medicare tax would also drop considerably. But if you make too much money, the strategy doesn't work because you would ultimately have to pay the higher taxes of the employer. You will also have extra accounting costs and incorporation charges and fees.

2. Maximize expenses to lower earnings. Consider giving employees gas cards as raises instead of higher wages. Or, you could provide lunch as a benefit.

3. Increase the amount of money you contribute into pension plans and other deferred compensation arrangements.

   Under certain circumstances, deferred compensation plans can be used to reduce your income and lower wages. These plans are considered wages (and thus included) at the *later of* (1) when the services are performed, or (2) when the employee's right to such amounts are no longer subject to a substantial risk of forfeiture [IRC Sec. 3121 (v)(2)]. This would mean you can't lose the money in the plan if you quit and are fully vested (there are other applicable rules as well). If there is a substantial risk that you will forfeit your pension, according to IRS rules, then when you retire, the amount of deferred compensation will be considered wages for the purposes of Social Security. This is advantageous because you delay or eliminate the tax if your income in the year you retire is below the taxable wage base (in 1995 it is $11,280). On the other hand, there's a good chance your income will still exceed this minimum. If that's the case, you have to decide whether it's worth postponing the payments on the tax.

   You might also be able to reduce what you owe for Social Security by *integrating your pension plan* (see next section).

4. Institute a medical payment program for illness and medical care. A bona fide program that pays these expenses or a portion of them is not included as wages for Social Security taxes.

Social Security integration

Section 401(c) of the Internal Revenue Code allows pension plans to integrate with Social Security. This integration allows employers to discriminate with regard to pension benefits for higher compensated employees. In the plan's view, Social Security diminishes as the pay goes up. If you can reduce an employee's benefits for the amount that Social Security would pay, it would be a higher percentage for lower paid individuals.

As pension plans and Social Security taxes have become more of a burden for employers, integrated pension plans have become more popular. There are many types of integrated plans but they all operate by the use of a formula that would reduce the pension benefits an employee normally would have received upon retirement by the amount of your Social Security benefit (or a percentage of it).

Many plans have set up an integrated plan with a "benefit goal." This means the pension plan sets a goal for the amount of money you will have upon retirement from a combination of your pension plan and Social Security benefits. The pension plan administrators establish this goal as a percentage of what your income was while you were working. For example, if it's determined that your benefit goal should be 70 percent of your income, the plan's administrator would calculate your Social Security benefits and then calculate the amount of pension you would receive. Therefore, if you have a defined benefit pension plan and your employer can reduce the amount that has to be funded for you as a result of your Social Security benefits, it will invariably cost the employer and the pension plan less money.

The intricate rules and technicalities vary widely. This section should serve only as an introduction. If you have specific questions, consult a pension expert.

Can you lose Social Security retirement benefits if you still work?

Unfortunately, when you work, you pay Social Security taxes and when you retire, you can lose benefits should you continue to work. Quite simply, most of us cannot afford to fully retire. Social Security benefits probably account for less than 40 percent of your retirement needs. It's really a contradiction: You work because you don't get enough in benefits, but if you work, you may lose more benefits.

After retiring, you may wish to work in some capacity. However, there is an *Earnings Limitation,* which means you can only earn a certain amount before you will lose your Social Security benefits. The sad truth is that the loss in Social Security retirement benefits is often almost what you would be earning in your new job. Your benefits will be reduced proportionately to what you make.

You need to understand the now infamous *retirement test.* Here are the rules:

For 1995, if you are between 65 and 69 years of age and your income is more than $11,280, your Social Security retirement benefits will be reduced by $1 in benefits for every $3 in earnings over $11,160. If you were between 65 and 70 years old between 1991-1994, the Earnings Limitation amounts are as follows:

Year	Age 65-70
1991	$9,720
1992	10,200
1993	10,560
1994	11,160
1995	11,280

If you are below age 65 for all of 1995, receive retirement benefits and have earned income over $8,160, you will have to give back an amount of your Social Security benefits equal to $1 of benefits for every $2 of earnings over $8,160. If you were under 65 years of age and were receiving Social Security benefits between the years of 1991-1994, the Earnings Limitation amounts are as follows:

Year	Under age 65
1991	$7,080
1992	$7,440
1993	$7,680
1994	$8,040
1995	$8,160

A Social Security recipient over age 70 who works during all the months of the year can earn any amount without loss of benefits.

It is important you understand these rules because these restrictions will probably determine whether you decide if it's worthwhile to work during your retirement. If you earn a maximum of $11,280 in 1995, you will not lose any benefits. But, if you earn more than $11,280, you will lose them. The figure of $11,280 increases every year with inflation. Remember, your earnings are only reduced for "earned income," which is income that you receive from employment, not from dividends or other sources of income.

There are some important exceptions to the Earnings Limitation rule:

1. In the year in which you retire, the amount you earn is figured monthly instead of annually. This could prove extremely beneficial if you can show a substantial amount of income concentrated in a few months, instead of spread throughout the year. Any *month*, instead of any year that you do not make the maximum amount allowable, you will receive your full benefits. If, for example, you concentrated your earnings into a few months, you would lose some money, but not as much as if you averaged it for the year.

2. For those of you turning 70 in that particular year, you need only to reduce your benefits for the months that you were under age 70. All income after the month you reach age 70 is free from reduction of Social Security benefits.

As you can see, working while "retired" can be costly. Let's do a few examples:

Example one

> You are 66 years old and are receiving Social Security benefits worth $10,000 per year. You work at the local hardware store for extra money. The total earned income in the current year will be $15,000. How much of your Social Security retirement benefits will be reduced?
>
> | | |
> |---|---|
> | $15,000 | Amount in earnings |
> | 11,280 | Withholding rate (amount allowed before benefits are reduced) |
> | (-) 3,720 | Excess income used to reduce Social Security benefits |
>
> $3,720 ÷ $3 = $1,240 (amount Social Security income will be reduced)

If you would have received $10,000 in Social Security benefits last year, after deductions, it will equal closer to $8,760 ($10,000 minus $1,240).

In this example, your Social Security benefits were shaved by over 10 percent. Technically, you were not earning $15,000 from your job because of the reductions in your benefits. You can see that it almost doesn't pay to work.

Example two

> Now let's assume that you are 64 years of age and have earned income of $20,000 and Social Security income of $9,000.
>
> | | |
> |---|---|
> | $20,000 | Earned income |
> | 8,160 | Withholding rate (amount allowed before benefits are reduced) |
> | (-) 11,840 | Excess income used to reduce Social Security benefits |
>
> $11,840 ÷ $2 = $5,920 (amount Social Security income will be reduced)

If you would have received $9,000 of Social Security income after the adjustment, you will now only receive $3,080.

What type of income is counted toward reducing your benefits?

Salary from an employer is the main sources of income that will reduce your benefits. If you are self-employed, it is net earnings. This would also include bonuses, commissions, fees—basically, any type of earned income.

Is there any income that is not counted as "earnings" for the Retirement Test?

Fortunately, some types of income are excluded from this test. Any earnings made after the age of 70 are not included. If you win a lawsuit, provided it is not for back pay, this money is also excluded. Also, investment income is not counted under the Social Security retirement test. (Note—this is not true for *taxation* of Social Security benefits. See section on taxation of Social Security benefits.) Retirement income from pensions and annuities is not included. Aside from those general rules, there are some specific applications:

1. Certain expense reimbursements related to an employee's hospitalization, sickness or death (spouses can apply too) are excluded. Usually this has to be under a planned system, so you should discuss setting up one with your employer. Since many retirees require medical care, instead of receiving a check, then having Social Security benefits reduced and then paying certain medical expenses, why not have your paycheck directly pay these expenses?

2. You can reduce income by contributing more to a retirement plan. These could include, depending on the level of employment, Individual Retirement Accounts (IRA) or Simplified Employee Pension plans (SEP, for the self-employed). If your company has a 401(k) plan, contribute to it. This will lower your income, which results in lowering your countable wages for Social Security purposes. There are even trickier rules related to nonqualified deferred compensation plans. If certain rules are followed, an employee or employer might be able to defer more income and then show lower wages. Ask your accountant to explain these rules if you think it may be appropriate in your situation.

3. If you need life insurance, you can set up a plan in which your employer purchases it on your behalf. There are many restrictions, including a maximum of $50,000 in death benefits, but it is something you should consider.

4. Utilize a plan whereby a portion of your wages is applied to the cost of your lunch. The meal must be at the employer's place of business in order for the meal's value to be excluded as wages.

All these factors should be considered as you're deciding whether or not you should take your Social Security benefits at the normal retirement age of 65, earlier at 62, or later after the age of 65. Chances are, if you think you will be working after "early retirement" and making more than the maximum amount that you are allowed to make before benefits are reduced (currently $8,160), it probably wouldn't make sense to take the benefits early.

Are there any people who do not have to participate in Social Security?

For the most part Social Security is compulsory, meaning you have to participate and, of course, pay the taxes associated with it.

However, certain workers such as railroad employees, state, local and federal employees may be covered under their own plans. The one other exception, may be the clergy. This includes rabbis, priests, ministers, certain members of religious orders and Christian Science practitioners.

The clergy are included in Social Security unless specific actions are taken to opt out. These people can claim exemption on the basis of conscientious or religious objections, or if they have taken a vow of poverty. Your place of worship must qualify as a religious organization. Then, you must inform your organization and submit a claim statement to Social Security.

Summary

It is astounding how little we know about it, given the amount of money spent on Social Security. All employers and employees should understand the system so that benefits can be maximized without adding unnecessary costs to anyone. Retired workers who receive benefits from Social Security should also know how the system operates so they can get all the benefits they should. By knowing how the system operates, you will learn what benefits you're entitled to and whether you can lose them if you continue to work.

Chapter 3

Determining your eligibility and your Social Security benefit rate

Summary of monthly benefit rates:

- Maximum monthly retirement benefit in 1995 $1,199
- Maximum benefit for spouse or child in 1995 $599
- Cost of living increase from 1995 2.8 percent
- The average monthly benefit for a retired worker $698
- The average monthly benefit for a retired couple $1,178

Requesting your Earnings and Benefits Statement from Social Security

As you may have guessed by now, I'm a big believer in planning. If you don't know approximately how much Social Security is going to pay you when you retire, you can't plan adequately for your retirement. Also, you may be surprised to learn that the Social Security Administration does make mistakes. After all, this agency is processing 200 million W-2 tax forms every year. That's why it's important you check prior to retirement to find out what you should receive in benefits so you'll know whether you're getting the correct amount. You want to be credited on all your earnings. Also be aware that there is Social Security fraud in which someone collects benefits based on someone's else's record and gets away with it. To avoid having someone tamper with your records, you should check your benefits record every three years.

Checking your benefits has never been easier. Fill out a *Request for Earnings And Benefit Estimate Statement* (Form SSA-7004) which is available at your local Social Security office or by phone (800-772-1213). A sample form can be found in this chapter. After you complete this form, you should send it to:

The Department of Health and Human Services
Social Security Administration
300 N. Greene St.
Baltimore, MD 21201-1581

What if there is an error in your Earnings and Benefit Statement?

You should immediately contact the Social Security Administration (800-772-1213) to explain the problem. If the error is simple, you may be able to resolve the problem over the phone. In this case, you should then request another Earnings and Benefit Statement to make certain the change has indeed been made. Routine errors include misspellings, wrong addresses, new married names, wrong date of birth, etc. More complicated problems occur if there's a mistake in your Social Security number or money that you earned is not included in your Social Security record. Again, you can call the toll-free number or your local Social Security branch office and ask for a for a complete history of your Social Security earnings. Be specific and request your entire record, not just your Benefits Statement. Be prepared to complete a lengthy form which asks detailed questions about previous earnings, pay a modest fee and then submit it with proof of the earnings in question.

You should follow these tips when you complete the form:

Print neatly or use a typewriter if possible. Double check that you write down the correct Social Security number and be as accurate as possible. When it comes to question #9 which deals with future earnings, you should add 5 to 10 percent to your current earnings. Your earnings will be indexed and will probably not affect the outcome either way.

In 1994, the maximum Social Security benefit a person could earn was $1,147 per month. In 1995, the maximum monthly payment was $1,199. Spouses and children can receive benefits as well. The maximum a covered employee and his or her spouse could receive would be $1,600.

Form Approved
OMB NO. 0960-0466

SP

Request for Earnings and Benefit Estimate Statement

Please print or type your answers. When you have completed the form, fold it and mail it to us.

1. Name shown on your Social Security card:

First Name _____ Middle Initial ____

Last Name Only _____

2. Your Social Security number as shown on your card:

☐☐☐ - ☐☐ - ☐☐☐☐

3. Your date of birth

Month ____ Day ____ Year ____

4. Other Social Security numbers you have used:

☐☐☐ - ☐☐ - ☐☐☐☐
☐☐☐ - ☐☐ - ☐☐☐☐

5. Your sex: ☐ Male ☐ Female

6. Other names you have used (*including a maiden name*): _____

For items 7 and 9 show only earnings covered by Social Security. Do NOT include wages from State, local or Federal Government employment that are NOT covered for Social Security or that are covered ONLY by Medicare.

7. Show your actual earnings (wages and/or net self-employment income) for last year and your estimated earnings for this year.

A. Last year's actual earnings: (*Dollars Only*)

$ ☐☐☐,☐☐☐.☐☐

B. This year's estimated earnings: (*Dollars Only*)

$ ☐☐☐,☐☐☐.☐☐

8. Show the age at which you plan to stop working.

☐☐ (*Show only one age*)

9. Below, show the average yearly amount (not your total future lifetime earnings) that you think you will earn between now and when you plan to stop working. Include cost-of-living, performance or scheduled pay increases or bonuses.

If you expect to earn significantly more or less in the future due to promotions, job changes, part-time work, or an absence from the work force, enter the amount that most closely reflects your future average yearly earnings.

If you don't expect any significant changes, show the same amount you are earning now (the amount in 7B).

Future average yearly earnings: (*Dollars Only*)

$ ☐☐☐,☐☐☐.☐☐

10. Address where you want us to send the statement.

Name _____

Street Address (Include Apt. No., P.O. Box, or Rural Route) _____

City _____ State ____ Zip Code _____

11. ☐ Please check this box if you want to get your statement in Spanish instead of English.

Notice:
I am asking for information about my own Social Security record or the record of a person I am authorized to represent. I understand that if I deliberately request information under false pretenses I may be guilty of a federal crime and could be fined and/or imprisoned. I authorize you to use a contractor to send the statement of earnings and benefit estimates to the person named in item 10.

Please sign your name (Do not print)

▲

Signature _____

Date _____ (Area Code) Daytime Telephone No. _____

Form SSA-7004-SM (5-94) Destroy prior editions   ♻ Printed on recycled paper

33

While it's important you request your Earnings and Benefits Estimate, you should also know how the SSA determines your benefits so you can check the numbers.

Steps to determine eligibility for Social Security

First step—determine insured status

As you would expect, there are many rules, restrictions and exceptions that determine whether you are "covered" or "insured" for various Social Security benefits. And, you must figure out whether your spouse, ex-spouse, widow or children are covered. You should divide your insured status into the following three broad categories: *fully insured, currently insured and insured for disability.*

To determine your insured status, the Social Security Administration uses *quarters of coverage.* As explained fully below, quarters of coverage refers to the time periods used by the Social Security Administration to calculate your benefits.

To receive full retirement benefits under Social Security, you need "40 quarters," basically 10 years, of coverage. (There are exceptions for disability and survivor's benefits.)

In 1995, employees received one quarter of coverage for each $630 of earnings, up to a maximum of four quarters. You usually have four quarters per year. Once your earnings reach the maximum amount for Social Security, no additional money counts. For the years prior to 1994, the same quarters of coverage applied but the dollar amounts were different.

Let's assume that you earned $2,520 in one month during 1995 and earned nothing else the rest of the year. You would have qualified for four quarters of coverage during that year {$2,520 ÷ 4 = 630 (the maximum allowed per quarter)}.

The following chart shows, for each year beginning in 1978, the amount in earnings necessary for you to earn a quarter of coverage. For example, if you earned $1,000 in 1978, you would have earned four quarters of coverage for Social Security eligibility benefits.

Earnings needed per quarter of coverage

Year	Amount	Year	Amount
1978	$250	1987	$460
1979	260	1988	470
1980	290	1989	500
1981	310	1990	520
1982	310	1991	540
1983	370	1992	570
1984	390	1993	590
1985	410	1994	620
1986	440	1995	630

Before 1978, the rules were a bit different. A quarter of coverage was based on any three-month period of a year beginning in January in which a worker received $50 or more in earnings for covered employment.

Figuring quarters of coverage for an employer and for a self-employed person is almost identical. But, for earnings prior to 1978, four quarters would be earned for a calendar year in which a person was credited with $400 or more of self-employment income.

What type of work counts for quarters of coverage?

1. Almost all work counts toward Social Security eligibility, as long as the work was performed in the U.S. If it was performed outside the U.S., it had to be for an American employer.
2. Federal employees are covered for the years worked after 1983.
3. Those serving in the armed forces on active duty are covered.
4. Employees of private, tax-exempt, nonprofit organizations are covered as of January 1, 1984 (including ministers and rabbis).
5. Spouses and many family members are covered.
6. Under certain conditions, state and local government employees are covered.

Type of work that does not qualify

1. Noncovered wages include retirement pay, employee expense reimbursements and payment by employers into annuity plans.
2. Employment in which you don't pay Social Security tax.
3. Certain periods during a disability.
4. Farm and agriculture employees.
5. Railroad employees are covered instead by the Railroad Retirement Act (many exceptions and restrictions apply).

How do you determine if you are fully insured, currently insured or insured for disability?

Fully insured

Fully insured means you are able to receive all the retirement benefits that you are entitled to under Social Security. You must meet at least one of two basic tests to be fully insured.

First, you need at least 40 quarters (10 years) of coverage. Once you have received 40 quarters you are insured for life.

You are fully insured if you have at least six quarters of coverage and have acquired at least as many quarters of coverage as there are years elapsing after

1950 (or later, after the year in which you reach age 21) and before the year in which you die, become disabled or reach age 62, whichever comes first. Any year that you had a disability does not have to be counted.

To summarize, you need one quarter for each year between the years of 1950 to the year in which you reach age 62. As confusing as this rule is, it can actually serve to reduce the number of quarters an older person must have to earn fully insured status for Social Security.

Assume Rachel applied for retirement benefits in 1980, the year in which she turned 65. She needed 26 quarters to be fully insured. There are 26 years between 1950 and 1977 (the year she turned age 62). Count the number of years starting *after* 1950 and *before she turned* age 62.

Currently insured

If you are currently insured, your survivors will receive certain benefits if you die before you are fully insured (see section on "Survivors' Benefits").

To be currently insured, a worker must have acquired at least six quarters within a 13-quarter period ending with the quarter in which the worker dies or becomes entitled to retirement or disability benefits.

Insured for disability

Other rules apply for Social Security Disability Benefits. If you become disabled between the ages of 24 and 31, you must have acquired at least six quarters in a 12-quarter period prior to becoming disabled. You must have earned these quarters in half of the quarters beginning with the quarter after the quarter in which you turned aged 21, and ending with the quarter in which you became disabled. The law does not say that you must earn these quarters consecutively; they can earned any time during the 40 quarter period.

If you become disabled at age 31 or older, you must have 20 quarters (five years) of coverage within a 40 quarter (10 year) period prior to becoming disabled.

How to determine your benefits

Now that you know the general rules used to determine if you're eligible for benefits, you must now figure out what the benefits are. This is a critical step in your financial plan. Knowing your Social Security benefits is as essential as determining your savings and the amount of your pension.

At either age 62 or 65, a fully insured worker is entitled to monthly income for the rest of his or her life. In addition, certain family members could also be entitled to "survivors' benefits."

The rules for receiving benefits are:

1. You *must* file an application within three months before the first month in which you become entitled to benefits (see appendix for sample application).

2. You must be fully insured.
3. You must have proof of identity and your age. Passports and birth certificates are usually acceptable forms of identification.
4. There is a *Maximum Family Benefit* (MFB) that could limit your benefits to a specified dollar amount even if you are entitled to further benefits. This often becomes a factor when more than one family member is entitled to benefits.

To figure your retirement benefits, several factors need to be considered. First, you must decide if you will take benefits at age 62 or 65, or any time in between (see section entitled "Should I take benefits at age 62 or 65?"). At age 65, you will receive full benefits. At age 62, you will receive 80 percent of the benefits.

Although the calculations to figure out what your benefits should be are difficult, it's important to work out the numbers so you can check the accuracy of your Social Security Administration records. The following topics will be broken down into two parts. Explained first are the basic formulas that you can use to determine the benefits on your own. This is the method that the Social Security Administration endorses and recommends you use to determine your benefits. Then, you will see a more complicated method using charts to figure out your benefits. While these calculations can be confusing, if you want a technical look at the government's method of determining benefits, you must follow each step.

Social Security figures your benefits using the following formula:

1. Earnings covered by Social Security are listed starting with the year 1951.
2. Earnings are adjusted for changes in average wages over the years. This means that your earnings for 1960 are considerably less than for 1994. Your earnings need to be *indexed* to reflect what those earnings will be equal to in today's dollars, adjusted for inflation. Earnings are adjusted for each year up until you reach the age of 60. Then, your actual earnings are used.
3. After you have created the list from step two, your highest earning years (from the mandatory 40 credits) are used to determine your benefits. (Usually 35 years are used.) If you are eligible for Social Security, but have not worked at least 35 years, a "zero" will automatically be added for all the years you did not work.
4. You will then take earnings from the previous steps, add them all up and divide by 420—the number of months in 35 years. This will give you a number called your *average monthly earnings* which is used to figure your benefit rate.
5. After you determine your benefit rate, you need to apply your average monthly earnings rate to a three-level formula in order to determine the exact amount of Social Security. This formula is

part of Social Security regulation. For example, if you were born in 1932, multiply the first $422 of your monthly earnings by 90 percent.

Then, multiply the next $2,123 of your earnings by 32 percent.

The remaining amount is multiplied by 15 percent. The result is then added together and should equal your basic full retirement age benefit rate.

The goal of this formula is to replace roughly 42 percent of a person's earnings. Obviously, this percentage would be lower for high-income individuals and higher for low-income individuals.

A new formula, with different numbers, is used each year. You can call the Social Security Administration to find out the new numbers, which are usually set in November.

How to figure your retirement benefits

If you start your benefits at normal retirement age, your benefits will equal your *Primary Insurance Amount (PIA)*. This is what monthly benefits are based on. If you don't start benefits at the normal retirement age, your benefits will be reduced by 5/9 of 1 percent (1/180) for each of the first 36 months you are younger than the normal retirement age. Essentially, this formula means that you'll receive 80 percent of your benefits at age 62.

That's a quick overview. Now comes the long answer with numbers and the technical definitions. Again, this may seem rather confusing but if you're interested in a precise calculation of your Social Security benefits, this is the method to follow. You should check the accuracy of your benefits even if you're already retired, not just if you're planning ahead.

Retirement benefits are almost always figured on the insured Social Security wages since 1950. Your benefits are directly related to your Primary Insurance Amount (PIA) up to a maximum amount which is defined as *Maximum Family Benefit*.

In the past, several ways of calculating your retirement benefits were used. Before 1979, the method of computation for benefits was called the Simplified Old-Start Benefit Method. Today, this method is used only if the insured employee becomes disabled, dies or reaches age 62 prior to 1979. This formula led to problems with the Cost of Living Adjustment (see section called "Notch Benefits"). Because of the COLA, the benefits could vary greatly, depending on the rate of inflation. These swings in benefits were not designed as part of the system.

After 1979, the *wage indexing* (otherwise known as *indexing*) method for computations of benefits took effect. With the wage indexing, your earnings are indexed for a fixed number of years after 1950. Basically, the formula lets you figure out the present value of your past earnings. This calculation is necessary because your past earnings are worth less because of inflation.

To calculate your benefits using the indexing method you must follow three steps:

1. Index the earnings record.
2. Determine the Average Indexed Monthly Earnings (AIME).
3. Apply the PIA formula to the AIME.

Indexing earnings—figuring your Average Indexed Monthly Earnings (AIME)

The *Average Indexed Monthly Earnings (AIME)* is the earnings record after wages have been indexed. You index to properly reflect what your actual earnings should be in the year in which you retire. When you calculate your AIME, index all years of earnings up to the "indexing year," which is the second year before you reach age 62, die or become disabled before age 62.

To do the calculation, you apply a ratio to your earnings for each year, starting in 1951. The ratio is the "indexing average wage" for the second year before the year of the worker's eligibility for benefits or death, divided by the "indexing average wage" for the year being indexed. The indexed earnings for each year are computed as follows:

The following chart will tell you the maximum taxable amount of earnings that you could credit toward your AIME when determining your Social Security benefits. (These are the maximum earnings you will be credited for annually.)

Year	Maximum allowable earnings
1995	$61,200
1994	60,600
1993	57,600
1992	55,500
1991	53,400
1990	51,300
1989	48,000
1988	45,000
1987	43,800
1986	42,000
1985	39,600
1984	37,800
1983	35,700

Year	Maximum allowable earnings
1982	32,400
1981	29,700
1980	25,900
1979	22,900
1978	17,700
1977	16,500
1976	15,300
1975	14,100
1974	13,200
1973	10,800
1972	9,000
1968 - 1971	7,800
1966 - 1967	6,600
1959 - 1965	4,800
1955 - 1958	4,200
1951 - 1954	3,600

The chart on page 41 will help you figure out your AIME. (Note: the numbers may vary slightly and should be rounded higher.)

Figuring your Average Indexed Monthly Earnings

1	2	3	4
Year	Taxable Earnings x	Index Factor =	Indexed Earnings
1951		8.26415	
1952		7.78008	
1953		7.36841	
1954		7.33058	
1955		7.00684	
1956		6.54879	
1957		6.35213	
1958		6.29666	
1959		5.99945	
1960		5.77289	
1961		5.66039	
1962		5.39047	
1963		5.26144	
1964		5.05486	
1965		4.96546	
1966		4.68428	
1967		4.43712	
1968		4.15177	
1969		3.92494	
1970		3.73937	
1971		3.56047	
1972		3.24269	
1973		3.05174	
1974		2.88051	
1975		2.68021	
1976		2.50720	
1977		2.36544	
1978		2.19142	
1979		2.01514	
1980		1.84862	
1981		1.67955	
1982		1.59192	
1983		1.51797	
1984		1.43369	
1985		1.37510	
1986		1.33546	
1987		1.25540	
1988		1.19647	
1989		1.15090	
1990		1.10009	
1991		1.06057	
1992		1.00860	
1993		1.00000	
1994		1.00000	
1995		1.00000	
1996+		1.00000	

Use the previous chart to complete the following steps

Step one

Get your earnings records for each applicable year. Put the earnings number in column #2. You can only use up to the maximum taxable amount as illustrated in the previous graph.

If you are having trouble recalling your taxable earnings for column three, you should get a Request for Earnings and Benefits Statement (as outlined earlier in this chapter). However, since the Social Security Administration does make errors, you should try and find the numbers in your own records.

Step two

Multiply your taxable earnings by the index factor to get your indexed earnings. For all years after 1995, to be on the safe side, simply use your actual earnings for 1995 or the earnings cap for 1995. This would probably most accurately reflect your AIME. Alternatively, you can increase the cap by 2 percent per year. By using the earnings cap for 1995, you should assume a 2 percent increase for subsequent years.

Step three

You must now determine how many and which years are the best ones to use.

Use the following table to figure how many years you need to figure out your Average Indexed Monthly Earnings (AIME).

Years required to figure AIME

Birth year	Number of years used to figure AIME
1925	31
1926	32
1927	33
1928	34
After 1928	35

The Social Security Administration figures out the amount of quarters of coverage you need to be fully insured for Social Security Retirement by using the *quarters of coverage test*. It states that quarters of coverage needed are determined by counting the number of years after you turn 21, through the year you reach age 61. If you were born before 1930, you would count the number of years after 1950 through the year you became 61. This number determines the quarters of coverage necessary for you to have fully insured status.

You can use the quarters of coverage test to determine AIME. To figure out how many years of earnings you must use for figuring your AIME, do the quarters of coverage test and figure out how many years are needed for fully insured status. Then, subtract five years from the number of years that are needed for you to be fully insured. This number will enable you to figure out your AIME.

Your chart should now be complete. Scan the indexed earnings column (column #4) and list all the highest earning years. Use the number of years required from the previous step. You can now disregard all of the previous years.

Step four

Take all the years that you have determined to be the highest and add up the Indexed Earning column from those years.

Since you want to figure out your AIME on a monthly basis, take the number of years you determined is needed for your AIME (from the quarters of coverage test) and multiply the number of years by 12 (amount of months in a year).

Step five

Take the total of your Indexed Earnings from the first part of step four and divide this number by the months you calculated in the second half of step four. This final step should give you your AIME.

Although this exercise will help you get a fairly close estimate of your AIME, the calculation is not 100 percent accurate. Also, if you were born 1933, a different calculation method was used. In addition, if you earned most of your income before 1951, you may qualify for a special calculation method which was used prior to the current system. Contact the Social Security Administration for this formula.

If you found the previous calculations difficult, you can do a quick "cheat" method. This chart already indexes the wages for specific years. These amounts must be used in 1995 to index earnings from 1951 through the indexing year.

Indexed earnings

Year	Indexed wages	Year	Indexed wages
1951	$2,799.16	1974	8,030.76
1952	2,973.32	1975	8,630.92
1953	3,139.44	1976	9,226.48
1954	3,155.64	1977	9,779.44
1955	3,301.44	1978	10,556.03
1956	3,532.36	1979	11,479.46
1957	3,641.72	1980	12,513.46
1958	3,673.80	1981	13,773.10
1959	3,855.80	1982	14,531.34

Year	Indexed wages	Year	Indexed wages
1960	4,007.12	1983	15,239.24
1961	4,086.76	1984	16,135.07
1962	4,291.40	1985	16,822.51
1963	4,396.64	1986	17,321.82
1964	4,576.32	1987	18,426.51
1965	4,658.72	1988	19,334.04
1966	4,938.36	1989	20,099.55
1967	5,213.44	1990	21,027.98
1968	5,571.76	1991	21,811.60
1969	5,893.76	1992	22,935.41
1970	6,186.24	1993	
1971	6,497.08		
1972	7,133.80		
1973	7,580.16		

Every year before November 1, the Department of Health and Human Services publishes the indexing average wage for the next indexing year. For example, the indexing average wage for 1993—the indexing year for those reaching age 62, dying or becoming disabled before age 62 in 1996, will be published no later than November 1995.

Review of how to determine your Average Indexed Monthly Earnings (AIME)

Determining your AIME is crucial. Without your AIME, it will be very difficult to determine your *Primary Insurance Amount (PIA),* or how much in benefits you will receive. When you're calculating your AIME, don't hesitate to call the Social Security Administration (800-772-1213) if you're missing any of your records. The Social Security Administration uses the earnings listed in your records, up to the annual wage limitation, to determine your AIME.

You can compute your AIME with the following steps, but it is a difficult process, so you may choose to use the approximate AIME charts included below.

1. Begin counting the number of years after 1950 (or beginning when you reached age 21 if it is later than 1950) and up to but not including the year you reach age 62. The number of years you count is the number of *elapsed years.*

2. Subtract five from the number of elapsed years. The resulting number is the number of computation base years to be used in computing the AIME (if two years or less use two).

   Please note that you only subtract the number five when figuring retirement benefits. Disability benefits are computed according to the worker's age. The numbers are as follows:

If you become disabled before you reach age 27, you subtract 0 years.

Disabled between 27-31, subtract one year.

Disabled between 32-36, subtract two years.

Disabled between 37-41, subtract three years.

Disabled between 42-46, subtract four years.

Disabled after 47, subtract five years.

3. Take your Social Security earnings in the "base years." Base years begin after 1950, and end the year before you are entitled to retirement or disability benefits or the year of death. Use the Maximum Earnings Limitations graph.

4. Index your earnings in each computation elapsed year, up to but not including the indexing year. Use the indexing charts and formulas.

5. Using the indexing of your earnings, and for years that your earnings are not indexed yet, select the years of highest earnings. This should be the same number you calculated in step 2. The years you chose need not be in any consecutive order.

6. The total of indexed and non-indexed earnings for the selected years are divided by the number of months in the number of years found in step 2. This is your AIME (Average Indexed Monthly Earnings).

The following is a table of your approximate AIME according to the year you were born and your earnings for 1994. The chart assumes a six percent annual pay raise through 1994 and then unchanged earnings until retirement.

AIME for Workers
Earning $15,000 - $35,000

Current Annual Earnings

Year Born	AIME	$15,000-$20,000	$20,000-$25,000	$26,000-$30,000	$31,000-$35,000
1932 (Age 62 in 1994)	Retirement	1,277	1,715	2,024	2,304
1933 - 1937	Retirement	1,303	1,750	2,069	2,382
1938 - 1942	Retirement	1,341	1,800	2,135	2,471
1943 - 1947	Retirement	1,380	1,853	2,203	2,557
1948 - 1952	Retirement	1,407	1,889	2,249	2,624
1953 - 1958	Retirement	1,430	1,920	2,287	2,681
1959 - 1964	Retirement	1,455	1,955	2,329	2,745
1965 (Under Age 30)	Retirement	1,458	1,958	2,333	2,750

AIME For Workers
Earning $36,000 - $60,000

Year Born	AIME	$36,000-$41,000	$41,000-$45,000	$46,000-$50,000	$51,000-$55,000	$56,000-$60,000
				Current Annual Earnings		
1932 (Age 62 in 1994)	Retirement	2,549	2,784	2,977	3,162	3,341
1933 - 1937	Retirement	2,662	2,933	3,162	3,382	3,597
1938 - 1942	Retirement	2,801	3,131	3,419	3,699	3,973
1943 - 1947	Retirement	2,931	3,307	3,649	4,000	3,436
1948 - 1952	Retirement	3,015	3,407	3,769	4,159	4,546
1953 - 1958	Retirement	3,084	3,488	3,878	4,282	4,685
1959 - 1964	Retirement	3,161	3,577	3,993	4,409	4,810
1965 (Under Age 30)	Retirement	3,166	3,583	4,000	4,416	4,833

Figuring your Primary Insurance Amount

After you have calculated your AIME, you can now calculate your *Primary Insurance Amount (PIA)*. Using the following chart, find the number in the first column that is closest to your AIME. The number should give you an amount close to your actual PIA.

Benefits for Workers		
Average Indexed Monthly Earnings (AIME)	Age-65 Retirement Benefit or Disability Benefit	Age-62 Retirement Benefit
	100% of PIA	80% of PIA
$800	$503	$402
$900	$535	$428
$1,000	$567	$453
$1,100	$599	$479
$1,200	$631	$504
$1,300	$663	$530
$1,400	$695	$556
$1,500	$727	$581
$1,600	$759	$607
$1,700	$791	$632
$1,800	$823	$658
$1,900	$855	$684
$2,000	$887	$709
$2,100	$919	$735
$2,200	$951	$760
$2,300	$983	$786
$2,500	$1,047	$837
$2,700	$1,088	$870
$2,900	$1,118	$894
$3,100	$1,148	$918
$3,300	$1,178	$942
$3,493	$1,207	$965

To calculate your own PIA, the rules are as follows:

PIA for those who are 62 in 1995

For those reaching age 62 in 1995 or becoming disabled (or dying) before reaching age 62 in 1995, the calculation to determine your PIA is relatively simple. The PIA is 90 percent of the first $426 of your AIME, plus 32 percent of the next $141 of your AIME, plus 15 percent of your AIME in excess of $2,567.

The actual PIA benefit amount determined by using the formula, as outlined above, must be increased annually for inflation, according to the Cost of Living Adjustments (COLA).

When you use this formula, you will arrive at a monthly benefit amount. To apply the COLA for the year you reach the age of 62, and all subsequent years, use the following chart:

Year	COLA
1987	4.2 percent
1988	4.0
1989	4.7
1990	5.4
1991	3.7
1992	3.0
1993	2.6
1994	2.8

If you reached age 62 before 1995, multiply the 1995 index factors in the above chart by the multiplier in the table below. These new factors will allow you to complete the above chart entitled "Figuring Your Monthly Indexed Earnings" by the index factor multiplier in the chart below. Use the new factors to finish the "Figuring Your Monthly Indexed Earnings" chart. Then you need to apply the appropriate PIA formula from the table below.

Year of birth	Index Factor Multiplier	PIA Benefit Formula		
		90%	**32%**	**15%**
1925	0.727219	First $310	Next $1,556	Over $1,866
1926	0.748803	319	1,603	1,922
1927	0.796558	339	1,705	2,044
1928	0.835789	356	1,789	2,145
1929	0.868882	370	1,860	2,230
1930	0.909017	387	1,946	2,333
1931	0.942892	401	2,019	2,420
1932	0.991473	422	2,123	2,545

Summary

Simply assuming that the Social Security Administration will have accurate records of our earnings and provide the right amount of benefits is the choice most of us make. However, no one should make this assumption. Although it may seem a burden to write for your records, check them and do time-consuming calculations to check your benefits, you should do so. After all, you're counting on your benefits to help you—perhaps providing 40 percent of your income—when you're retired. You should take a little extra effort to check that your records are accurate and you'll be getting all the benefits you deserve. The first step is so easy: Get a copy of your Earnings and Benefits form from the Social Security Administration. With this information, you can then spend an hour or two doing your calculations. Taking a little extra time and effort today can have payoffs for many years ahead!

Chapter 4

Social Security procedures and important tips

What procedure should you follow when you are ready to receive Social Security checks?

You should apply for Social Security benefits three months prior to your retirement date. Even if you don't have all of the documents, you should still apply for benefits. You may be able to submit these documents later on or the Social Security Administration may be able to help you obtain them.

Documents needed in order to apply for Social Security

1. Social Security card.
2. Birth certificate.
3. A tax return if you are self-employed or a recent W-2 tax form if you are an employee.
4. Driver's license.
5. Proof of citizenship.
6. Marriage certificate (if you are using your spouse's record).

When do you receive Social Security checks?

Social Security checks are issued to you by the Treasury Department. The checks are usually delivered on the third day of the month following the month for which the payment is due.

Can your check be mailed directly to a bank or brokerage account?

You can have your check deposited directly into an account. By doing so, your check is more likely to get to an institution on time. Also, you're less likely to have your checks lost or stolen. When you fill out the forms to begin your Social Security benefits, you're asked whether you want your check automatically deposited. Even if you haven't chosen this option, you can later have your checks automatically deposited by calling Social Security's toll-free phone line or fill out the form (SF-1199) indicating where you would like the check sent. Write legibly and make sure you have the correct address. You should select a bank branch that is most convenient for you. Ask your financial institution whether you can have your check mailed to another branch, even if you do business at one location.

Direct-deposit for Social Security and other checks is advantageous for several reasons. There is less paper wasted and Social Security saves money. Also, there's less chance of fraudulent uses of checks.

What happens if you move?

Immediately visit your local Social Security office or contact the office by telephone. You can fill out a "change of address" form or write a note including your former address, new address and Social Security number.

What if you do not receive a check?

Contact the Social Security Administration immediately so that a replacement check can be issued (which shouldn't take longer than 30 days). You should also ask your local post office manager whether there have been problems with any other missing checks.

What should be done when a person dies?

In most cases when someone dies, his or her beneficiaries will be entitled to benefits. The beneficiaries should file an application for beneficiary benefits as soon after the recipient's death as possible. If there are several people eligible for benefits, each person must fill out a separate form.

The beneficiary also must complete another form in order to receive the lump-sum death benefit. The beneficiary has two years to complete this form.

What happens if the person receiving Social Security benefits becomes incapacitated?

The Social Security Administration allows for direct deposit of checks authorized by a power of attorney in these cases. You will have to complete the Authorization for Deposit of Social Security Payments Form (1199).

You should have prudent powers of attorney and durable powers of attorney drafted *now* while you are still capable. You should designate a spouse, trusted family member or friend. If you are nervous about giving powers of attorney for all your financial affairs, make it specific for limited actions, such as deposit of Social Security checks.

What if you start receiving benefits and then return to work?

If you feel that you will earn more than what you are allowed before reductions are made to your Social Security benefits, contact Social Security and explain the situation. Most likely, you will have to complete an estimated earnings form. You should be aware that if you fail to notify Social Security, not only can future benefits be deducted, but you could be subject to a penalty for not "promptly notifying Social Security."

What are the current monthly earnings limits?

In 1995 the maximum amount an individual could earn was $1,199 per month. If the Social Security beneficiary was married, the couple's benefits would probably be just over $1,600. The spouse is usually entitled to roughly 50 percent of the covered spouse's benefits but that can be reduced by the *Maximum Family Benefit*.

Maximum Family Benefit (MFB)

This rule places a maximum amount on how much in benefits a family, survivors and dependents can receive. The rule also applies for benefits paid on the work record of a disabled worker. It's important to find out what your MFB is. Your MFB can be found on your Earnings and Benefits Statement which is available from the Social Security Administration.

The rule simply states that if all the benefits that a worker and the worker's dependents are entitled to do not exceed the maximum family benefit, the worker's benefits will be paid in full. However, all the other benefits paid on that worker's record are reduced proportionately to the maximum allowable under the maximum family benefit.

The family members' (dependents', survivors') benefits are figured as a percentage of the worker's Primary Insurance Amount (PIA). The MFB is calculated by using a gradual percentage of the PIA. Since the MFB is calculated using a person's PIA, each person will have a different Maximum Family Benefit. Historically the MFB ranges between 150 and 180 percent of your PIA.

The MFB for those who are going to be age 62 in 1995, or dying before they reach age 62 in 1995, is 150 percent of the first $544 of PIA, plus 272 percent of the next $241, plus 134 percent of the next $239, plus 175 percent of PIA in excess of $1,024.

If you're disabled, the Maximum Family Benefit is calculated differently. It is the smaller of either 150 percent of PIA or 85 percent of the AIME, but not less than the PIA.

Minimum Benefit

Social Security also protects those people who worked but made very little money. The *Minimum Benefits Rule* applies so that no matter how much you earned, if you are fully insured, you will receive a specified minimum amount. The formula for PIA for minimum coverage is based predominantly on length of work. The formula is as follows:

If you worked between 1937 and 1950 you would divide your total earnings by $900 to obtain your years of coverage. The maximum is 14. If you worked between 1951 and 1978, you are credited for each year that you earned at least 25 percent of the Maximum Taxable Earnings (see Maximum Taxable Earnings chart in this chapter). For work between 1979 and 1990, you would be credited for each year that you earned 19 percent of the Maximum Taxable Earnings. After 1990, you need roughly 11 percent of the Maximum Taxable Earnings to be credited.

If you are trying to determine the special minimum PIA for 1995, it would probably be just under $26 per month for *each year of coverage* over 10 years, but only up to a maximum of 30 years.

What is a notch baby?

Social Security benefits increase each year, with an inflation rider, legislated by Congress in 1972. But with inflation in the double digits during the late 1970s, Congress got nervous and in 1977, enacted a new system designed to slow the amount that would be paid to Social Security recipients. This new formula led to a dramatic reduction in benefits. For example, a person born in 1920 who retires at age 65 would get a monthly check of 10 to 20 percent less than that of someone born in 1916. In fact, if you were born between 1917 and 1926 and retired at age 65, you would probably receive less than people retiring before and after you.

This "notch" in benefits affects more than 12 million retired workers (and spouses) in the United States. Congress is currently studying the "notch" problem to decide whether the retirees in the "notch period" receive too little in benefits or whether earlier Social Security recipients are getting too much. The debate continues.

Will Social Security benefits stay fixed once you begin receiving benefits?

The Social Security system is set up to pay you a bit more money every year. This increase is the *Cost of Living Adjustment (COLA)*. The COLA is usually figured using the rise in the *Consumer Price Index*. Known as the CPI, this is a measure used to help determine the inflation rate. But, some members of Congress have suggested eliminating the COLA as a way to save money.

When will you be eligible for benefits in the future?

The *Normal Retirement Age* is presently age 65. However, the Normal Retirement Age will increase, beginning in the year 2000. In the year 2027, the Normal Retirement Age will be age 67. The formula for retirement age will be increased by two months a year for workers reaching age 62 in the years 2000 to 2005 to age 66 and so on. Everyone born after 1938 will be affected by these changes.

The reasoning behind these changes is that the life expectancy was much shorter when Social Security was first created. However, since people are now living longer, the SSA is afraid that these extra years will wipe out the fund and Social Security will go broke. Note: Medicare benefits will still begin at age 65.

What should you do if you think that you should be receiving a larger Social Security check?

The good news is you have a right to appeal any decision. By either contacting your local Social Security office or calling the toll-free number (800-728-8901), you can obtain a *request for appeal* form. There are rules about when to submit the form and who will review it. The procedure usually is as follows:

1. File a written appeal on the appropriate form.
2. Wait for an initial determination to be made.
3. If you disagree with the initial determination you can ask for a reconsideration.
4. If reconsideration is granted, you may be granted your request or the case may be sent to an Administrative Hearing.
5. The final step is the Appeals Council Review. Usually the claimant, his or her representative or any other interested party is not invited to this closed session. This decision is usually the highest one. The Appeals Council can reverse any earlier decision, but very rarely can an Appeals Council decision be overturned.
6. You could also try to get a Judicial Review, if you can get a U.S. Federal District court to hear the case (if a court thinks you have a good case and you can prepare a strong brief).

Summary

The information in this chapter about applying for Social Security and the rules governing lost checks, direct deposit, earnings limits and other aspects of your benefits is designed to help you utilize the system more easily. By reviewing this chapter, you will be able to move ahead in the system quickly with a minimum of hassles. It may seem obvious but knowing the procedures will enable you to cope with what can be an overwhelming bureaucracy. Not only will you save time but you should be able to receive benefits promptly and file an appeal if you feel you're entitled to more benefits.

Chapter 5

When to take Social Security benefits and taxation of retirement benefits

Should you take your benefits at age 62, 65 or later?

The question of whether to take Social Security benefits when you reach age 62, 65 or older is a good one. Unfortunately, there is no easy answer to this question. You should consider many factors including:

1. Are you going to work after your retire? If you earn too much, your Social Security benefits will be reduced.

2. Are you a savvy investor? If you don't need the money at age 62 and can invest it, you may accumulate more money in the long run.

3. Do you need other social services such as government aid or Medicaid? To qualify for some of these programs, it may be preferable to show less monthly income. If you take benefits before you reach the Normal Retirement Age of 65, you will receive less in monthly benefits.

If you retire at age 65—the Normal Retirement Age—and are fully insured, you will receive 100 percent of your Primary Insurance Amount (PIA) and you will get full benefits.

If you take benefits prior to age 65, your benefits will be reduced by roughly 5/9 of 1 percent for every month that you take the benefits. The earliest you can take your benefits is when you reach age 62. At age 62, your benefits will be reduced to 80 percent of what you would have received at Normal Retirement Age.

You can also "retire" *after* age 65. Usually, this doesn't make much sense, unless you are working after retirement. If you reached age 65 before January 1, 1982 you would receive an extra 1 percent per year until you reach age 72. If you waited to receive benefits until age 72, you would get an extra 7 percent more than if you took benefits at Normal Retirement Age.

For those of you who turned 65 between January 1, 1982 and December 31, 1989, your benefits will increase by 3 percent for each year you delay retirement. However, this increase stops when you turn 70. If you waited and took benefits at 70, you'd receive 15 percent more than if you took benefits at Normal Retirement Age. Assuming you don't need the money, you can calculate if it pays to wait.

If you were to receive $10,000 per year in benefits (assuming an annual inflation increase), assuming you retire at age 65, between the ages of 65 and 70 you would receive $50,000. If you wait to take benefits when you turn 70, you will get $11,500 per year (with an inflation increase) instead of $10,000 per year.

Assume you don't need the money if you can wait to receive benefits until you turn 70. If you took the $10,000 per year and invested it conservatively, you could earn 6 percent. In five years, when you reach 70, you would have more than $56,500. Now, assume that you start withdrawing income out of the account equal to the 6 percent rate of return. The income equals $3,390 per year, more than twice the extra $1,150 you would have received by waiting to take benefits at age 70. *Plus*, you still have the principal of $56,500 in the account. There is one additional consideration. If you have income prior to the age 70 but take benefits at age 65, your benefits will be reduced. You will have to evaluate the amount your benefits will be reduced to determine whether it's worth taking the benefits at age 65.

The reverse is true if you're considering taking benefits at age 62. Without considering earned income or taxes, you probably want to have the money in your pocket. Although you would only be receiving 80 percent of the Normal Retirement benefits by taking them at age 62, you would be able to save quite a bit. If you receive $10,000 per year at 65 years of age, then you would get roughly $8,000 at age 62. If you could afford to wait until age 65, then you could save the money Social Security provides between ages 62 and 65. If, at 62 you get $8,000 per year and invest it at 6 percent until the time you reach age 65 in three years, you would have saved about $25,500. If you continue to take the income equal to 6 percent, that will total more than $1,500—almost as much as the $10,000, the amount you would have received by waiting until age 65. And, you still have the $25,000 in your pocket. And, if you're an astute investor, you can get more than a 65 percent return on your money. You should ask yourself whether you're able to manage the money better than the Social Security Administration. Of course you must consider a negative scenario as well. The Social Security money might be spent improperly, depending on any credit problems you end up having.

If you work after you retire, it sometimes makes sense to delay taking your benefits. If you take them, the benefits will be reduced if you earn over a certain amount and you will also have to pay tax. However, you shouldn't delay taking Social Security benefits later than age 70. When you reach age 70, you aren't subject to any income limits. You're also receiving close to the maximum amount you could receive. There's no advantage to not taking the benefits at this age.

Tax on Social Security benefits

Your benefits are subject to tax. Not only do you pay into the Social Security system and your benefits are reduced when you work after you retire, but your Social Security benefits can be taxed as well.

What are the threshold amounts of income subject to tax on Social Security benefits?

Single, or married filing separately (and not living together)

Income	Tax Rate
Income more than $25,000 and less than $34,000	50 percent of Social Security benefits are taxable
Income more than $34,000	85 percent of Social Security benefits are subject to tax

Married filing jointly

$32,000	50 percent of benefits are taxable
$44,000	85 percent of benefits are taxable

This means that a portion of your Social Security income is taxed and must be reported as income on your taxes. You will have to do some calculations to figure out how much of your benefits will be taxed.

First, you take your *Adjusted Gross Income (AGI)* on your 1040 tax form, and add back any tax-free interest from bonds that you have received during the year. (Although you may assume your tax free bonds are really tax free; for Social Security purposes, they are part of your income) This amount is your *Modified Adjusted Gross Income (MAGI).* Remember, Adjusted Gross Income (AGI)+ tax free income = MAGI. Finally, you have to add your *Social Security benefits to* your income. The amount you pay taxes on is determined by *the lesser* of either 50 percent of your total Social Security benefits or 50 percent of the difference between the sum of your MAGI, plus 50 percent of your Social Security benefits.

Example: Assume you are married, filing jointly. In 1994 you had Adjusted Gross Income (as listed on your 1040 tax form) of $25,000. You and your spouse also have combined Social Security benefits equal to $12,000. In addition, you have a municipal bond mutual fund that paid tax-free interest last year of $8,000. Are your Social Security benefits going to be taxed? Yes. Here is how the taxes are figured:

$25,000	Adjusted Gross Income
6,000*	50 percent of your Social Security benefits
8,000	Tax-free interest
33,000	Modified Adjusted Gross Income (MAGI)

*$6,000 is the lesser of: 50 percent of your Social Security benefits or 50 percent of the difference between your MAGI ($33,000) plus half the Social Security ($6,000) = $39,000 less your base ($32,000) = $7,000. The lesser, in this case, is half the Social Security benefits.

The amount of tax on Social Security benefits will be calculated by taxing 50 percent of the *excess* over the first threshold ($32,000). In this case, only $1,000 is over the first threshold. This amount is then added to the adjusted gross income.

If the couple's Modified Adjusted Gross Income was $65,000, with $20,000 in Social Security benefits, they would pay tax on 50 percent of the Social Security benefits above the first threshold ($32,000). Then, they would pay an additional 35 percent tax, totaling 85 percent over the next threshold ($44,000).

Are there ways of reducing your Modified Adjusted Gross Income to reduce the taxes you pay on your Social Security benefits?

If you're savvy enough to plan in advance, you can find some ways to constructively reduce your income for Social Security purposes. The best way to reduce income is to make sure you "shelter" income you don't need so it will not show up as "income" according to Social Security regulations. Here are some ideas:

1. Certain annuities defer income you do not withdraw from the annuity, so a properly structured annuity can help reduce your income.

You cannot receive a 1099 tax form from the annuity. You can usually invest in a variety of investment vehicles from fixed accounts to mutual funds.

Do your homework when you research these annuities. Check ratings, penalties, fees and whether or not you ever have to annuitize. (I prefer deferred annuities that do not require annuitization and I discuss these in my book, *Senior Savvy*).

2. Don't cash in IRAs and other pensions until absolutely necessary. Many people think that once they turn age 59½ they have to begin withdrawing IRA or other pension money. You can begin to withdraw without paying an early withdrawal penalty but it usually pays to delay taking pension or IRA distributions for as long as possible. You must begin taking withdrawals at age 70½. It pays to determine how much to withdraw carefully. There are several ways to figure your *Required Minimum Distribution (RMD)* to reduce the amount you have to withdraw. The less you have to withdraw, the lower your income will be. If you recalculate your life expectancy every year, you will probably reduce the amount you must take from an IRA. Consider naming a younger person such as a child as beneficiary. By doing so, you can, up to a point, combine your own and the child's mortality to arrive at a lower Required Minimum Distribution.

3. Make certain you maximize all of your deductions. Match proper losses to gains and take investment losses in order to reduce your income. You may even sell a stock that you think will stay depressed and buy it back after 31 days.

4. Many retirees, widows and survivors are eligible for tax-credits such as the elderly person's tax credit, tax for disability or blindness and low income tax credits. Taking advantage of these credits, can reduce your taxable income for Social Security purposes.

Summary

Each of you will have to determine when is the best time to take your Social Security retirement benefits. You'll have to carefully weigh your need for the money with several factors such as whether you plan to continue working and your tax liability. It's essential that you plan before you take your benefits so you don't end up making a decision that will cost you money in the years ahead. Do your calculations before making a decision so that you can maximize your benefits.

Chapter 6

Spousal, family and survivors' benefits

A key purpose of Social Security is to provide benefits to spouses, widows and other family members. This chapter will focus on these benefits.

- The average monthly benefit for an eligible widow (young) with two eligible children is $1,365.
- The average monthly benefit for an eligible (aged) widow without children is $656.
- Spouses will receive 50 percent of covered workers' benefits at the normal retirement age.
- Spouses who receive benefits at age 62 will receive 37.5 percent of covered workers' benefits at normal retirement age.

All of these extra benefits are probably going to be subject to the Maximum Family Benefit rule (see applicable section).

Spousal benefits

Definition of a spouse

In general, a spouse, for purposes of Social Security, is someone who is legally married to an insured person and is the natural parent of the insured person's child. The spouse must have been married to the insured person for at least one year prior to the day on which the insured's application for benefits are filed. (There are exceptions, as well as additional rules.)

There is some variation because of the state laws. Most states do not recognize common-law marriages. If you are considering a second marriage and are worried that your "significant other" will be left poverty stricken without your Social Security benefits, you may want to consider a marriage. Unfortunately, the reverse is true with regard to other benefits. If you're worried about protecting assets from Medicaid, for example, you may not want to be married. Review your state law and consider the consequences of a marriage on your benefits.

Spousal benefits have been the subject of much debate with some consumer organizations and women's groups arguing that their benefits aren't equal to those received by men. There is a simple explanation for this discrepancy in benefits: The Social Security system was created on the premise that men were the primary earners and far fewer women were in the work force. Women who leave the workforce to care for children will simply not accumulate the same number of hours as a man who worked continuously throughout his career. Often, a woman's benefits are almost as low as what someone would get without having worked. Often, women end up relying on their husbands' benefits. But this can pose a problem if the couple divorces within 10 years of marriage. Furthermore, disabled widows who need benefits prior to retirement age will receive severely reduced benefits.

There are other inadequacies as well: If only one spouse works, when he or she dies, the surviving spouse receives two-thirds of the couple's combined benefits. If both spouses earned Social Security benefits, the survivor receives only the larger of the two benefits.

Spouses of eligible workers can receive retirement benefits. The benefits depend on whether the eligible worker is *fully insured or currently insured* (see previous chapter). The following are the ways spouses are compensated:

1. The spouse of a fully insured worker is entitled to half of the spouse's basic benefit at age 65 or older. The spouse can begin to take benefits at age 62 but the benefits will be reduced. It could be reduced to as low as 37.5 percent of their spouse's basic benefit.

2. The spouse can take the benefit prior to age 62 if either spouse is taking care of an entitled child—one who is under age 16 or disabled. The benefit will not be reduced even if the spouse is under 65.

3. The spouse of an eligible worker has a choice. If he or she is entitled to his or her own Social Security benefits *greater* than half of those of the spouse, he or she can take the larger benefit.

Remember, although you may be entitled to receive Social Security benefits from your own work record, taking your spousal benefits may provide you with more benefits. Check with the Social Security Administration for an estimate of your benefits and those of your spouse.

Survivors' benefits

Widow(ers) and other family members are entitled to benefits if certain criteria are met:

1. Surviving spouses age 60 or over are entitled to benefits if the deceased spouse was fully or currently insured. If the spouse is between the ages of 50 and 60 he or she may qualify for benefits if he or she is disabled.

2. The rule of thumb is that the widow is entitled to 100 percent of benefits at Normal Retirement Age (65) as long as the deceased spouse was entitled to 100 percent of benefits. If a deceased spouse was receiving benefits at his or her time of death, the widow(er) is entitled to receive these same benefits.

3. If the surviving spouse wishes to take benefits prior to age 65, the benefits will be reduced by roughly .475 percent of the benefit amount for each month the benefits are received prior to age 65. The earliest eligible age is age 60. The benefit would equal roughly 71.5 percent of what the person would have received at age 65.

4. It's important that you check with Social Security to find out whether your survivorship benefits are higher than your own Social Security benefits. Widows may also be entitled to Medicare if their spouses would have been entitled to monthly benefits or had worked long enough under Social Security.

5. The rule states that if you were married at least 10 years prior to the previous spouse's death and have not remarried at the time you are applying for benefits, you are entitled to the same benefits as a surviving spouse (see previous section).

6. Widows with children under the age of 16 are usually entitled to benefits earlier than age 60.

7. Also, divorced widows and widowers may be entitled to some benefits from an ex-husband or wife even if the surviving ex-spouse is remarried. Usually, full benefits are made to widow(ers) at age 65 regardless of a remarriage.

Do divorced spouses get benefits from living ex-spouses?

Yes, provided you meet the following criteria:

• Your marriage lasted at least 10 years.
• The divorced spouse is a covered worker.
• The divorced spouse must be at least 62 years of age.

If the couple has been divorced for two or more years, the divorced spouse is entitled to benefits even if the insured worker has not yet retired.

Obviously, if the ex-spouse's Social Security benefits are higher than his or her own earnings, the benefits will first be based on his or her own records. If your income were so small that you'd receive more based on your ex-spouse's record, you could receive a portion of your ex-spouse's benefits up to a maximum amount. However, if you were married twice before, you would not be entitled to benefits from both ex-husbands. You have the option of choosing from which ex-spouse you want to receive benefits. Obviously, it would make sense to choose the spouse with the highest Social Security benefit. Although there are some exceptions, as a general rule, if you do remarry, you usually cannot get benefits from a divorced husband or wife. One exception is if the spouse does remarry, that person can still claim benefits if they marry a person receiving Social Security benefits as a widow, widower parent or disabled child.

If you have dependent children or grandchildren

For Social Security purposes, a dependent child is one who has a continuing disability that began before the child turned age 22, or one who is under the age of 18 (19 if he or she is still a full time high school student). This rule applies to adopted children, biological children, stepchildren, grandchildren and great-grandchildren. As long as the insured worker is caring for the child, this child would be entitled to benefits.

The amount the child will receive is equal to 50 percent of the retired (or disabled) worker's benefits for each child (subject to family maximum).

If the eligible worker dies, the dependent child will receive 75 percent of that worker's benefit (subject to family maximum). If both parents die, the child has the right to take the highest benefit. When the child marries, the benefits will stop.

Children's benefits

For Social Security purposes, children are defined as: any legitimate or illegitimate biological children, adopted children, stepchildren and, in most cases, dependent grandchildren.

To receive benefits, a child must be under age 18. If the child is 18 he or she must be in high school, or the child can be any age if disabled before age 22.

Parents' benefits

It is also important to note that parents of Social Security recipients may be eligible for benefits. If the insured worker dies and that person had been the parents' principal means of support, the parents should be entitled to benefits. The parents must be age 62 or older to receive these benefits.

Lump-sum death benefit

If a worker dies and was currently or fully insured at the time of death, a one-time payment of $255 is payable to a surviving spouse, regardless of the worker's or the spouse's age. If there is no surviving spouse, children may receive this benefit if they are eligible for a benefit on the worker's record. You must file a claim for this benefit within two years of a worker's death.

Examples to clarify these types of benefits:

Assume that Richard and Jane are married. Jane is age 65 and has never worked. However, Richard is fully insured under Social Security and receives $900 per month (disregard any Maximum Family Benefits for these examples).

How much is Jane entitled to at age 65?

Jane is entitled to 50 percent of her husband's base amount. In this case it would equal $450.

What if Jane was age 62 and wanted to take benefits, could she?

Jane could take benefits between ages 62 and 65. The amount Jane would receive is reduced by a formula down to the minimum at age 62 which is 37.5 percent. In this case Jane would receive $337.50 as a monthly retirement benefit.

Again, what if Jane was 65 but also fully insured under Social Security and eligible for $400 per month.
How much would she receive on a monthly basis?

Jane would receive $450 per month—$400 which is the maximum amount of her separate benefits and $50 from her spouse's benefits. Remember, spouses are entitled to half of their spouse's benefits.

Summary

The Social Security benefits available for survivors, children and other family benefits are a very helpful resource for these families. This chapter provides a brief introduction to family benefits but there are also many specific rules that are not covered here. If you think you're eligible for these benefits, make sure you contact your local Social Security office or call the toll-free number. Don't overlook your family's Maximum Family Benefit. To find out this amount, get your Benefits and Earnings Statement from the Social Security Administration.

Chapter 7

Determining disability benefits for eligible workers and their families

You worked for the last 10 years and then were involved in an accident that caused a total disability. How are you going to pay the bills? How will you replace your lost earnings? Do you think Social Security will—although you are not yet "fully insured" for retirement benefits? Fortunately, there is a good chance that Social Security will provide you with some benefits. This chapter will help you determine your eligibility for Social Security disability benefits.

Congressional representatives felt eligible workers and their families should have coverage in the event the worker suffered a disability. And, the odds of someone suffering a disability are astronomically high. In fact, on average, a 45-year-old has about a 1 in 8 chance of suffering a disability compared to a 1 in 88 chance of being in a fire. The average disability for this person is roughly 3.4 years. The average monthly benefit for a disabled worker is $661. If you are between the ages of 45 and 65 and currently earn $3,000 per month, you stand to lose $720,000 in loss of earnings for that period if you're disabled. For this reason, the Social Security Disability program provides help in difficult times. (For more information on disability, read my book *Safeguard Your Hard-Earned Savings*.)

The primary issue is that the Social Security Administration defines disability differently than you or I would.

There are two separate types of disability programs. They are the *Supplemental Security Income (SSI)* and *Social Security Disability Insurance*. This chapter deals with the latter, *Disability Insurance Benefits (DIB)*; this program is also known as Title II benefits of the Social Security Act. The aim of DIB is to provide monthly benefits to workers and other eligible recipients, if they become disabled.

Requirements to receive disability benefits

1. You must be able to meet the definition of disabled, according to Social Security. Disability is an inability to engage in any substantial gainful activity by reason of a medically determinable physical or mental impairment which is expected to result in death or which has lasted or can be expected to last for a continuous period of not less than 12 months (see "Disability Requirements").
2. You must be fully insured to receive disability insurance (see "Fully Insured" section in Chapter 3).

There is a difference between being fully insured for retirement benefits and fully insured for disability benefits. To be fully insured for disability purposes, you need to work at least five of the 10 years prior to becoming disabled. This means you must have worked at least 20 quarters in the 40 quarter period ending in or after the quarter, or on the onset of disability.

Requirements for disability benefits based on insured status

Born after 1929, become disabled at age	Credits you need
31 through 42	20
44	22
46	24
48	26
50	28
52	30
54	32
56	34
58	36
60	38
62 or older	40

If, for example, you worked regularly from 1960 until 1990 and then stopped working because of a disability, you would have disability insured status for 10 years after 1990—40 quarters or 10 years.

If you become disabled before you reach age 31, the rule is modified to one-half of the quarters between the quarter after the one in which the worker reached age 21 and the quarter of the onset of the disability. However, the minimum is six quarters of coverage.

If you become disabled before age 24, you need six quarters of coverage in the 12 quarter period ending with the quarter you become disabled.

3. There is a five month waiting period from when you apply to when you receive Disability Insurance Benefits (DIB).
4. Families and dependents may receive benefits (see section on "disability benefits for workers' families, ex-spouses, children and other survivors").
5. Certain disabilities that do not fall under the previous definition can be covered.
6. Disability benefits are for anyone who is disabled, regardless of income or assets. You can even have a spouse actively working and still receive the benefits. This is different than Supplemental Security Income (SSI), which is based on need.

A further definition of disability requirements

The Department of Health and Human Services has set up a rigorous evaluation system to determine if you are truly disabled. If at any point they feel you are not disabled, the evaluation is stopped and you are not granted DIB. The process is as follows:

1. You cannot perform any substantial or gainful work due to a medically determined physical or mental impairment that is expected to result in death, or that has lasted or can be expected to last continuously for at least 12 months.

   In some cases you're expected to try to work. Occasionally, you are permitted to try to work while receiving disability insurance.
2. Your disability must be *severe*. This means that because of a physical or mental condition, your ability to perform any work is significantly limited. In many cases there are lists of impairments that are considered disabilities.
3. If you can't return to your previous job but are able to perform in gainful capacity in another vocation, you may not qualify, or may receive a trial disability period. If you're age 55 or older, you're expected to do work comparable to what you've done previously.

Special rules for blindness

The program makes it easier for blind persons to receive DIB. To be considered blind, your vision cannot be corrected to better than 20/200 or tunnel vision.

A blind person does not need to meet the 20 out of 40 quarters test. However, to be covered, blind individuals must be fully insured.

Disability benefits for workers' families, ex-spouses, children and other survivors

The same rules used for retirement benefits apply for family benefits. Rules are strict for divorcees. You can receive benefits, but in most cases, if you remarry you will lose the benefits.

As a fully insured worker's survivor, the family is entitled to disability benefits. This is true even if the deceased worker was not entitled to disability benefits. Also, if a surviving family member is disabled, the individual may be paid disability benefits earlier or longer than he or she normally would have received for survivor's benefits. To be eligible as a disabled family member (widow, divorced spouse, etc.), the individual must meet the same disability test as the workers who attain age 50 must meet.

Disabled widow(er)

If the widow(er) is age 50 or older and was married to a now deceased individual who either received disability or was fully insured, then the survivor is eligible for benefits. If the widow(er) remarries before age 50 or before the onset of disability, he or she will not be entitled to disability widow benefits.

The survivor must have been married to the deceased person for at least nine months prior to the worker's death or be the mother or father of the worker's child.

Child benefits

If a child is a dependent of a deceased worker, the child can be eligible for benefits even if the worker was not eligible for benefits at the time of death. The worker needs to be fully insured, or covered by Social Security for at least six of the 13 quarters immediately preceding disability or death.

The child must be under age 18, or a full-time student under age 19. The child must be disabled and have been disabled prior to his or her 22nd birthday.

How much money can you get in disability payments?

This answer varies from individual to individual, depending on the circumstances.

To determine benefits, you would normally figure out what the disabled person's Primary Insurance Amount (PIA) would be at either normal retirement age, or at the time the disability occurred. However, the formula used to determine your Primary Insurance Amount, and Average Indexed Monthly Earnings (AIME) is different for calculating a disabled benefit.

Also, a disability benefit will end when you reach retirement age and will receive normal Social Security benefits, or when your disability ceases or when you die. The Social Security Administration does not want you to be "awarded" by receiving more money for a disability. To prevent the total amount that a family can receive from all entitlement sources, there is a Maximum Family Benefit (see appropriate section).

If you wish to figure out your own disability retirement benefits, you have a few options. One option is to complete the Request for Earnings and Benefits Form (see appendix). This tells you how Social Security works. You can also approximate your benefits. This is done the same way you figured out your retirement benefits in Chapter Three. Use the following as a guide:

The amount you will receive as a disability benefit will be your Primary Insurance Amount (PIA) at the time of the disability. To figure your PIA you must first know your Average Indexed Monthly Earnings (AIME).

If you were born after 1993, you can use the following chart (note this chart is the same one used to figure AIME in Chapter Three). Enter your taxable earnings for all years including the year you became disabled. If your earnings were more than the limit for Social Security purposes in any year, you must put down the maximum earnings countable for Social Security. If you do not know the maximum earnings in any year refer to the graph entitled "Maximum Earnings" (in Chapter Three). After your earnings are inputted, multiply the earnings by the factor in column three of the chart.

Now figure out how many years are usable to determine your AIME. Consult the following chart, find your year of birth and look at the corresponding number of years. That is the number of years used to figure your AIME (should you wish to know why that number of years is used refer to the AIME rule in Chapter Three). Once you have found the number of years, multiply by 12 to get months.

Number of Years Used To Figure Average Indexed Monthly Earnings

Year of Birth	Number of Years	Year of Birth	Number of Years
1930-33	35	1953	16
1934	34	1954	16
1935	33	1955	15
1936	32	1956	14
1937	31	1957	13
1938	30	1958	12
1939	29	1959	12
1940	28	1960	11
1941	27	1961	10
1942	26	1962	9
1943	25	1963	8
1944	24	1964	8
1945	23	1965	7
1946	22	1966	6
1947	21	1967	5
1948	20	1968	4
1949	20	1969	4
1950	19	1970	3
1951	18	after 1970	2
1952	17		

Figuring Your Average Indexed Monthly Earnings

1	2	3	4
Year	Taxable Earnings x	Index Factor =	Indexed Earnings
1951		8.26415	
1952		7.78008	
1953		7.36841	
1954		7.33058	
1955		7.00684	
1956		6.54879	
1957		6.35213	
1958		6.29666	
1959		5.99945	
1960		5.77289	
1961		5.66039	
1962		5.39047	
1963		5.26144	
1964		5.05486	
1965		4.96546	
1966		4.68428	
1967		4.43712	
1968		4.15177	
1969		3.92494	
1970		3.73937	
1971		3.56047	
1972		3.24269	
1973		3.05174	
1974		2.88051	
1975		2.68021	
1976		2.50720	
1977		2.36544	
1978		2.19142	
1979		2.01514	
1980		1.84862	
1981		1.67955	
1982		1.59192	
1983		1.51797	
1984		1.43369	
1985		1.37510	
1986		1.33546	
1987		1.25540	
1988		1.19647	
1989		1.15090	
1990		1.10009	
1991		1.06057	
1992		1.00860	
1993		1.00000	
1994		1.00000	
1995		1.00000	
1996+		1.00000	

Once you have found the number of years necessary for the AIME calculation, refer back to the chart "Figuring Your Average Indexed Earnings." Circle each of the highest years in column four until you satisfy the number of years required from the previous step. Add up all the indexed earnings that you have just circled as being the highest earnings for the number of years required.

Divide the total earnings from the previous step by the number of months and you should have your AIME.

Note: You may be able to reduce the number of years further. The rule is: If you become disabled after the age of 24, but before age 37, you may reduce the number of years needed for an AIME calculation by one for each year in which a child of yours or your spouse's under the age of three lives in your house and if you were not employed (up to a maximum of two years if you are age 26-31 and by one year if you are age 25 or age 32-36).

Once you figure your AIME, figure your Primary Insurance Amount (PIA).

If you become disabled in 1995, refer to the chart below. Find the number in the first column that is closest to your AIME. Follow along until you find your approximate PIA.

Benefits for Workers		
Average Indexed Monthly Earnings (AIME)	Age-65 Retirement Benefit or Disability Benefit	Age-62 Retirement Benefit
	100% of PIA	80% of PIA
$800	$503	$402
$900	$535	$428
$1,000	$567	$453
$1,100	$599	$479
$1,200	$631	$504
$1,300	$663	$530
$1,400	$695	$556
$1,500	$727	$581
$1,600	$759	$607
$1,700	$791	$632
$1,800	$823	$658
$1,900	$855	$684
$2,000	$887	$709
$2,100	$919	$735
$2,200	$951	$760
$2,300	$983	$786
$2,500	$1,047	$837
$2,700	$1,088	$870
$2,900	$1,118	$894
$3,100	$1,148	$918
$3,300	$1,178	$942
$3,493	$1,207	$965

How to file a claim for disability

1. Send a written request to the Social Security Administration stating your intent to file for disability benefits. If you follow up the written notification within 60 days with a disability application, the Social Security Administration will use the date of the first written inquiry as the application date.

2. Complete a Disability Benefits Application Form (SSA-16) and file it with your district or branch office, listed in your yellow pages under U.S. Government services. The application is complex and may take some time, so you should get started immediately.

3. There is a five-month waiting period from the onset of the disability before the disability benefit will be paid. To qualify for the benefits you must have been disabled for the entire five months.

    The waiting period rule does not apply if you were disabled five years prior to your current disability.

4. Your local or district SSA office will determine if you are fully or currently insured for disability status.

    If you are deemed ineligible based on insured status (before a review of your disability), you will have 60 days to request a review of this determination and submit additional evidence.

5. If you do pass the insured status, your file will be forwarded to the state agency responsible for determining if you are disabled. This office is known as a *State Disability Determination Service* and is responsible for determining whether or not you are disabled.

You will be interviewed by the State Disability Determination Service before it makes its decision. You will be required to supply evidence and documentation from many sources. Be prepared to provide, at a minimum:

- Your Social Security card, birth certificate and sometimes driver's license.

- Your medical records/files, hospitalization dates and log of doctor visits and details on why you went to the doctor or entered the hospital, how long you stayed, the location, prescriptions, etc.

- A detailed history of your work including the name of your employer, how long you have been employed, what your specific job duties are and how your disability has affected those duties.

- The State Disability Determination Service will then request and verify medical records. They will probably have you examined by an approved medical professional.

It is critical that you do everything you possibly can to help your case. Make sure your doctors are sending the medical records requested. The best thing you can do is to send as much supporting documentation with the application and have it available for the interview. When you originally file you might include evidence:

1. If you have been found disabled by other agencies, or by workers' compensation, etc.
2. Letters from previous employers and/or co-workers.
3. Statements from family members and people you live with about how the disability has impaired or affected your life.

Do not give the Social Security Administration any original documentation. Make copies and send certified mail (return receipt). If you are working with a local office ask the person who takes your information to give you a receipt for the information. Far too often, information is lost.

Once all the information is assimilated and reviewed, the State Disability Determination Service will notify the *Office of Disability Operations* of its decision. This office administers the disability programs for the SSA. It reviews the state agencies' determination, provides ongoing investigations, conducts reviews, etc.

The Social Security Administration makes a practice of reviewing at least 65 percent of all the state agency determinations. The SSA has the discretion to deny coverage to anyone.

What if you are denied disability insurance?

You should absolutely appeal the decision. You have 60 days from when you receive your denial notice to ask for reconsideration.

If your reconsideration appeal is again denied, you should request a hearing. You have 60 days from receiving notice that your reconsideration appeal has been denied to request a hearing. You must file form HA-501 with your district office. You are usually given notice 20 days prior to the hearing and you should receive your hearing date within three to six months after filing for it.

Unfortunately, having a hearing is almost like starting over. You prove that you are disabled and insured for disability benefits. You should review your Social Security file prior to the hearing in order to prepare yourself. You should hear the outcome of the hearing roughly three to 10 weeks after the proceedings. You can contact the local *Office of Hearing and Appeals (OHA)* if you have not heard about the decision of your hearing within three to six months. You can also contact the national office (5107 Leesburg Pike, Falls Church, VA 22041; 703-756-9106).

Appeals process in a nutshell

1. Reconsideration.
2. Hearing by an administrative law judge.
3. Review by the Appeals Council.
4. Federal court review.

After receiving disability benefits, you will continually be reviewed

It's important to understand that after you start receiving disability benefits (as well as SSI benefits), your case will be continually reviewed. This review process is designed to show whether you are still disabled.

In borderline disability cases, where a recovery is expected, you will receive a review within the first six to 18 months. If the disability is expected to be permanent but a recovery is possible, your case will probably be reviewed every three years. If a recovery or improvement is not expected, your case will probably be reviewed about every five to seven years.

You think you might be able to work again, but don't want to risk your benefits if you're unable to work

Social Security has a trial work program. You must notify the Social Security Administration of any work attempts and you can continue receiving disability benefits for nine months after you begin working. After nine months an additional three month grace period will further extend your benefits, after which benefits are usually suspended. Any month with earnings exceeding $200 is considered work.

Benefits can be reinstated during a 36-month extended period of eligibility for any month that earnings do not exceed $500.

Summary

While you may prefer to think that you won't suffer a disability and don't have to worry about your financial situation if you're unable to work, this is simply an unrealistic situation. Disability is a far more common situation than you realize. All too many people who suffer a disability don't have sufficient funds to sustain their standard of living. Getting disability coverage through Social Security is not easy and, even if Social Security pays you a disability benefit, the benefit often doesn't cover all your expenses. Still, if you are entitled to disability benefits, you should carefully follow the application procedure. And, if you're denied benefits, you should appeal. Remember, too, that disability coverage isn't awarded on a one-time permanent basis. You may qualify for disability coverage now, but at some point in the future Social Security could deny your benefits if it determines that you are able to work. To avoid serious financial hardship, you should review your employer's disability policy. If you're not employed or if the coverage is inadequate, you should consider getting private disability insurance.

Chapter 8

Supplemental Security Income (SSI)

1995 Supplemental Security Income figures

Federal benefit rate: Individual	$458 per month
Federal benefit rate: Eligible couple	$687 per month
Essential person increment: Individual	$223 per month

Of all the Social Security and other entitlement programs (entitlement meaning that because you paid into the system, you're entitled to some benefit), the *Supplemental Security Income (SSI)* program is most similar to welfare. Eligibility requirements and benefits differ from Social Security programs described earlier.

SSI is federally financed and administered by the Social Security Administration (SSA). Designed to provide a monthly cash benefit to people who qualify (usually they're disabled, low-income or blind), its goal is to insure a national minimum level of income. About 4.5 million people in the U.S. receive SSI benefits.

While SSI shares similarities with Social Security Disability Insurance, there are significant differences. There are four broad requirements for eligibility.

Maximum Family Benefits for 1995

Monthly maximum	Individual	Couple
Basic federal payment	$ 458	$ 687
Income limits:		
Earned income	$1,001	$1,459
Unearned income	$ 478	$ 707
Asset limits (annual)	$2,000	$3,000

Main requirements for SSI eligibility

1. **Age.** You must be 65 years of age or older, blind or disabled. The definition of an adult who is disabled is very similar to the Disability definition for Social Security Disability Insurance Benefits. Essentially, SSI looks at whether you can function independently, appropriately and effectively in an age-appropriate manner.

   A child under 18 is disabled if he or she has any medically determinable physical or mental impairment which does not allow him or her to function as a nondisabled person of the same age would.

2. **Medical condition.** You may qualify if you are blind (defined the same for Social Security Disability Insurance).

3. **Citizenship and residency requirements.** You must be living in the United States, which includes Northern Mariana Islands but not Puerto Rico. You must also be a citizen of the United States or an alien lawfully admitted for permanent residence or permanently residing in the United States under that legal definition.

4. **Income and asset test.** You have countable income (and income not counted), as well as countable assets. In 1994, singles were allowed countable earned income up to $977, or $466 of unearned income, per month. A couple living alone in a private household was allowed to earn $1,423 (of earned income) or $689 of unearned income.

   In terms of assets (or resources, as SSI refers to them), individuals are allowed to have $2,000 or less and married couples, $3,000 or less.

The first three steps are fairly straightforward. The income and asset test is the one subject requirement subject to discussion, particularly for parents. Parents who create a trust or leave money to a disabled child often worry whether the child will still be able to qualify for SSI.

Countable and noncountable income and assets to determine SSI income test

As shown in the chart on the previous page, there is a maximum amount of unearned and nonearned income for single and married couples. You should understand what constitutes both types of income.

Countable income

1. All sources of money received. This includes income in any currency, checks or anything else representing income, such as gold. If you are given things such as food, clothing and shelter in lieu of

money, these items are countable income, but items arranged through barter or trade are not countable income.

2. All earned income. Income earned in a work program at a care facility is counted.
3. All unearned income. This could include but is not limited to Veterans' Benefits, Workers' Compensation, alimony, pensions, gifts, interest, annuities, dividends, rents, royalties, etc.

Noncountable income

1. The first $20 you receive from a source, except public assistance.
2. The first $65 per month of earned income.
3. One-half of all your earned income over $65 a month.
4. Irregular income from gifts or dividends up to $20 per month.
5. Housing assistance from a federal housing program.
6. Food stamps.
7. Work-related expenses for blind or disabled persons which are paid for through public assistance.
8. Amounts from tuition and fees paid from grants and fellowships.
9. Impairment-related work expenses.

Countable assets

1. Any real estate and fixtures on it excluding personal residences.
2. Personal property including homes, furnishings, jewelry, etc.
3. Anything broadly defined as investments. This includes bank accounts, checking accounts, etc.

Noncountable assets

1. Your personal residence as long as you are living there.
2. Personal property worth up to $2,000.
3. One car.
4. The cash value of life insurance worth $1,500 or less.
5. Income producing property regardless of its value as long as it is used for a trade or business and is essential to your support. For example, a carpenter's tools would be noncountable. However, if you have income producing property, then you are probably producing income and therefore may be ineligible for SSI.
6. Any property, items or resources approved as self-support mechanisms because of a disability.
7. The $6,000/6 percent rule. The SSA will exclude up to $6,000 of the equity value of non-business property used to produced goods

or services that are essential to daily activities. However, the property must have a net annual return equal to at least 6 percent of the excluded equity value of the property. If the return is less than 6 percent, then this exclusion only applies if the lower return is due to circumstances beyond the individual's control such as illness and there is the expectation that the property will again produce a 6 percent return.

What is interesting is that the income and asset tests for SSI are very similar to those of other programs such as Medicaid. Roughly the same methodology is used for various entitlement programs because you essentially have to be poverty stricken in order to qualify. However, the savvy individual can appear "broke" on paper, but in fact, can shelter other assets.

Can a child receiving SSI benefits receive an inheritance or gift without losing the benefits?

As you might expect, it is very difficult for a child to keep his or her benefits in this situation. It's probably easier for you to gift someone assets than gift them income. The income rules are rather inflexible but the asset rules offer room for interpretation. The following suggestions are offered by some elder care specialists but, as with all individual situations, you should seek counsel from an elder care attorney familiar with estate rules in your state as well as disability and elder care law. You should bear in mind that the rules differ from state to state and change almost daily. Consider the following advice only as a means to introduce you to possible strategies for gifts. Do consult a specialist if you are writing your will or establishing a trust.

Trusts have been the predominant means of giving children assets without causing them to lose their SSI benefits. This strategy has worked because the trust recipient—the child—doesn't presently have the assets, does not receive the income and does not have access to the funds. Therefore, the trust is not part of the included assets. If the SSI beneficiary does receive any of the trust income, the income would be included in the SSI recipient's income at that time.

However, there have been a number of legal cases where the establishment of a trust did not protect the child's benefit status. If your adviser recommends you establish a trust, ask the person several times whether he or she has used the identical trust for other people in the same situation. There's no point in establishing a trust that doesn't achieve what you want.

Irrevocability of the trusts is the key to this strategy. A *Medicaid Qualifying Trust* is a popular name of a trust that works to *disqualify* you for Medicaid, but could be beneficial for people receiving SSI benefits. *Special Needs Trusts, Offshore Trusts, Craven Trusts, Disability Trusts* are all popular names of trusts that people have used in one way or another to help protect SSI benefits for individuals who currently receive benefits or may have received them in the past.

You may want to create a trust in conjunction with a judicial proceeding. For example, you can go to court to prove that the individual is incompetent and needs a guardian or conservator. In this case, the trust is not voluntarily created by the person receiving SSI benefits, but the court creates the trust.

How the trusts are created is also significant. Often, what works to protect SSI benefits does not work to protect assets with regard to Medicaid. This is critical since SSI usually goes hand-in-hand with Medicaid benefits. You don't want to qualify for one and disqualify yourself for the other.

Medicaid and SSI have similar asset and income limitations. But, a major difference is that SSI does not have stringent rules governing how you give away money prior to receiving SSI benefits. SSI recipients can transfer money at any time without restriction prior to applying for SSI benefits. On the other hand, Medicaid has strict rules known as the *look-back rules* or 36-month rule, etc. You have to remember that when you get advice for one program to find out the ramifications if you end up needing the other program as well.

Although fancy estate planning tools can work for some people, you can also consider a simpler approach. If you have a disabled child and another child who is not disabled, you can leave your estate to the non-disabled child and have a verbal agreement that the disabled child is his or her responsibility. You concern would be that if the well child is sued, gets divorced or otherwise has financial difficulties, that he or she may use the money intended for the disabled child. To handle this situation, you could establish some type of irrevocable trust arrangement, or a lifetime benefit, with spend-thrift provisions. This would make it difficult for the well-child's spouse to deplete the trust for any reason.

Don't confuse Social Security Disability Insurance with Supplemental Social Security Income (SSI)

It is important to point out that in the Social Security Disability program, assets or other income are not factors in determining benefits. To receive SSI, your income and assets must not exceed a certain level but you don't need work experience. In the Social Security Disability program, your eligibility is determined primarily by your past work experience.

How much can I get from Supplemental Security Income (SSI)?

The basic federal payment for a single person in 1995 is $458 a month, or $687 for a couple. As with most federal programs, these amounts usually increase every year, at a rate tied to the Consumer Price Index (CPI). However, the amounts received vary for a number of reasons including:

1. Whether you or your spouse has other income.
2. Whether you live with your children and don't contribute to household expenses.
3. Whether anyone else is providing you with any means of support.

Also, some states have their own benefits that could increase your total monthly benefits.

Applying for SSI

You can apply for SSI in person at your local Social Security office or by sending in a "request for benefits" form. Obviously, you will need your Social Security card, as well as proof of identity and age such as your birth certificate, driver's license or passport. You will also need to provide a great deal of income information related to your assets including bank accounts and mortgage.

Since SSI can be crucial to you, don't hesitate in getting help with your application. There are many free or low cost agencies that will assist you (see Chapter 14 for a list of these agencies).

As with other decisions involving Social Security or the Health Care Financing Administration, you have the right to an appeal if you are denied SSI. Appeal forms are available at your local Social Security office. Help with the appeal form and the appeals process is available from the aforementioned agencies.

Summary

The Supplemental Social Security program offers great benefits. Unfortunately, the program is burdened by its own bureaucracy as well as the often confusing rules. Getting SSI can be a difficult experience but if you arm yourself with up-to-date information, seek expert counsel and are persistent, you should get benefits if you meet the eligibility requirements. Don't hesitate to appeal and try again if you're denied benefits.

Chapter 9

Exceptions, services and women and Social Security

Federal employees

Most federal employees are covered by either the Federal Employment Retirement System (FERS) or the Civil Service Retirement System (CSRS). If you fall into this category, you should review your benefits material to get information on these programs.

Some government employees who receive government pensions are also eligible for Social Security benefits as spouses or widows (widowers). In these cases, the employees are subject to a government pension offset. This rule means that if you receive a government pension, your benefits will be reduced by two-thirds of your government pension. For example, if you had a government pension of $500, your spousal Social Security benefit would be reduced by approximately $334.

Military employees/veterans

Veterans and families of veterans may be entitled to certain benefits without having to qualify under the standard rules.

Active military employees have two different types of retirement plans, depending on whether they became active before or after 1986. This text will not explain in detail military benefits; however, members of the military should inquire at their local Veterans' Affairs office.

In addition to any military benefits for which you qualify, you may receive Social Security benefits as well. After 1957, military personnel were included in the Social Security system with a rate of about $300 for each calendar quarter.

If you were employed in the military between 1940 and 1956, you would have received one quarter of Social Security coverage for each of the calendar quarters while you were on active duty. For each month of service, $160 in earnings would be credited to your Social Security account. You should note that you received this credit even though the Social Security taxes were not withheld from your paycheck. However, if you are receiving a federal pension over the allowable limit (check the current annual limit at your local federal employees government office), you will probably not receive these Social Security benefits.

Family members of veterans may be entitled to benefits even if the worker was not fully insured under Social Security. There are several programs that offer benefits to survivors of veterans who were killed while on active service or in service-connected incidents. Contact the Veterans Administration (1-800-827-1000) for details about these programs.

Railroad workers

Railroad workers are also covered under a separate program. Most railroad employees are covered under the Railroad Retirement Act. Generally, if a railroad worker has worked for 10 years, he or she is entitled to some type of retirement or disability coverage.

As with the military and federal employees, there are many specific rules about disability benefits, survivor benefits, retirement taxes and other regulations that apply to railroad workers. You can get information on these rules from the local federal employees government office.

Americans who worked in other countries

Many U.S. citizens presently work or have worked in foreign countries and contributed to those countries' Social Security systems. To be eligible for benefits in the country that you worked in, that country must have what is known as a *totalization agreement*. Countries that have this benefit include:

Austria, Germany, Italy, Switzerland, Norway, the Netherlands, Belgium, France, Canada, Portugal, Spain, Sweden and the United Kingdom.

Finland, Luxembourg and Ireland are expected to be included in 1996.

In addition, if you were part of a foreign program and have not worked in the United States for 10 years, you may still be eligible for Social Security benefits in the United States.

Employees of private, tax-exempt, nonprofit organizations

As of January 1, 1994, all employees of tax-exempt institutions are covered. There are special rules for clergy if they wish to opt out or take a vow of poverty.

Domestic employees

If you employ someone in your home over the age of 18 and pay that person more than $1,000 per year, his or her wages are subject to Social Security and Medicare payroll taxes.

Agricultural laborers

Most agricultural laborers are covered by Social Security. Only payments made in cash are counted. In addition, the employer must either spend more than $2,500 a year for this work or more than $150 to each employer each year.

Family employees

If you're self-employed, you may hire family members to work with you in the business. The Social Security regulations apply in this situation as well. If you hire a spouse, parent or child (18 years or older) you must treat the person like any other employee and make the appropriate withholdings for Social Security.

Are Social Security benefits reduced if you make too much money?

Yes. There are several ways that Social Security income may be reduced. There is a Maximum Family Benefit that applies if several family members are receiving various benefits and the family unit's total income exceeds certain limits. Also, if you go back to work during your retirement, you may exceed Social Security income limits. (See section entitled "Can I lose my Social Security benefits if I still work?" in Chapter 2).

How benefits from other pension plans impact Social Security benefits

If you are covered under Social Security *and* you are receiving money from "noncovered" earnings, your Social Security benefits will probably be reduced. Usually, noncovered earnings are defined as certain earnings that result from federal employment and other specific types of earnings that are not covered under Social Security.

There are exceptions to this rule. They include:

1. Individuals reaching age 62 before 1986.
2. People eligible for such pensions prior to 1986.
3. The beneficiaries of a worker who was disabled prior to 1986.
4. People who are eligible for Social Security who are at the Minimum Retirement Benefit levels.
5. Federal employees who were mandatorily covered by Social Security on January 1, 1984 and were not covered prior to that time.
6. People employed on January 1, 1984 by nonprofit organizations who were not covered by Social Security prior to 1984.

Many government workers from the federal level to the local county level were not covered by Social Security before they retired from service. Many state and local employers, for example, "opt out" of Social Security and provide an alternative to Social Security. However, many of these employees have had previous jobs or later take jobs that qualify them for Social Security benefits. If you fall into this category, two-thirds of your pension benefits from that employment will be offset against any Social Security benefit for which you are eligible. You may be eligible as a covered employee from a subsequent job, your spouse or as a widow or widower but you can only receive the amount of Social Security benefit that *exceeds* two-thirds of your government pension. Unfortunately, this often means that you won't receive any Social Security benefits.

Again, there are some exceptions, including:

1. People entitled to Social Security benefits before December 1977.
2. Individuals who were dependent on their spouses who received or were eligible to receive government pensions from December 1977 to November 1982.

Homemakers can lose out on death disability payments

Social Security provides disability coverage for insured workers. However, if you are out of the work force for five years or longer, you will probably lose your disability coverage. Let's assume that you are a homemaker taking care of the children. If you became disabled, it would seriously impact your family. Your husband is working and covered under Social Security Disability, but you, as a "non-working" spouse will probably lose your disability coverage. And, unfortunately, if you, the mother, die, your children probably would not be eligible for survivor benefits under your coverage.

Can homemakers and other part-time workers protect their benefits?

You do not need much in wages to receive a credit of Social Security. In fact, all you need is one quarter per year. In 1995, to receive one quarter of credit for Social Security, you need to make $630. You should think about what you could do in order to earn this amount of money. If you work part-time, ask your employer for an additional project. If you have a hobby or skill that could generate some income, look for jobs to do so. For example, if you have word-processing skills, put an ad in the local paper offering to type resumes or reports.

How are women impacted by Social Security?

Technically women are not treated differently. But it sometimes appears that they are. Here's a rather common situation:

You're a woman who's working and contributing to the Social Security system. However, when you have children, you leave the work force for several years. By interrupting your working years, you are reducing your periods of credit applied to your benefits. Perhaps you had been working for several years prior to having your children, but if you don't return to the workforce later on, you may never be fully insured. That's how women are paid far less in benefits than men who work for continuous years without taking time off. This is one of the inequities of the Social Security system.

Summary

The Social Security system is an extensive system of benefits. Specific rules govern virtually everyone so you and your family are treated differently than your neighbors. Among the factors determining both your eligibility and your benefits are your age, previous employment and family income. To take full advantage of your benefits, you should understand the system and plan your working years to make sure you earn as many credits as necessary for you to qualify for benefits.

Chapter 10

Introduction to Medicare

Important Medicare statistics

- Medicare Part A premium: Free to fully insured Social Security workers age 65 or older
- Medicare Part A premium for workers with 30+ quarters: $183 (in 1995)
- Medicare Part A deductible: $716
- Medicare Part B monthly premium: $46.10

What is Medicare?

In addition to retirement benefits and disability insurance, the government also established a universal health care system for everyone reaching age 65, covered by Social Security. This system is Medicare, the federal health insurance program. However, Medicare has become far more complex and costly than the lawmakers originally anticipated.

The system is so involved that often it takes a Medicare specialist to make certain you are receiving all that you are entitled to. Even before getting into the specifics of the programs, one generalization is worth making: Nothing about Medicare is simple. You must learn to read between the lines and be prepared to appeal in order to get your benefits. For example: Medicare will not pay for most preventative medical techniques such as routine physicals. But, there are ways that you can have Medicare pay for most of your physical examinations. Read on to find out how.

Don't confuse Medicare with Medicaid. *Medicare* is available to everyone who is age 65 and fully insured under the Social Security rules (see applicable section in this text). Medicare is a type of medical insurance. *Medicaid* is an entitlement or welfare program that you may be eligible for if you have no savings.

It's easy to lump the two programs together, because Medicare does not cover many of the large medical expenses you will have during retirement. Medicare rarely pays for nursing home stays and Medicaid will pay only if you're poverty stricken. It may be unfair but that's the way the system works. Your best defense is to arm yourself with as much information as possible so that you can protect your financial security. No one wants to go broke during retirement. For more information on this important subject, you can consult my book, *Safeguard Your Hard-Earned Savings*.

It's also worth mentioning that Medicare pays for less than half of your medical expenses during retirement. That's why it's so important that you get the Medicare coverage that best suits your needs. It also means that you should learn about Medicare supplements and Health Maintenance Organizations (HMOs) because you will probably be using these services as well.

How health care bills are paid

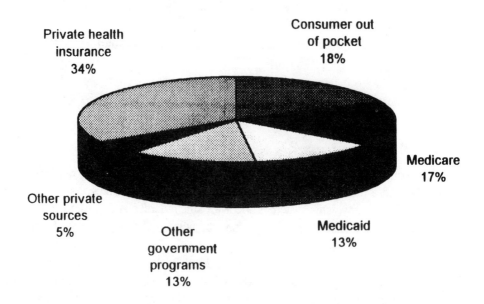

Private health insurance 34%

Consumer out of pocket 18%

Medicare 17%

Other private sources 5%

Other government programs 13%

Medicaid 13%

How do I get my Medicare card?

Three months before your 65th birthday, you should go to your local Social Security Administration office. You will complete an application for Medicare and then receive the basic information. Ask for the *Medicare Handbook,* which will give you an adequate outline of Medicare's services, what is and is not covered and appropriate amounts for the applicable year. Within the next two or three months, you should receive your Medicare card, which you need to carry at all times. Keep copies of the card in your safe deposit box.

What department administers Medicare?

Medicare is administered by the Health Care Financing Administration (HCFA), part of the Department of Health and Human Services. The Social Security Administration processes Medicare applications and claims, but it does not set Medicare policy. HCFA sets the policies and the standards by which doctors, hospitals, hospices and other organizations must meet in order to be authorized as qualified Medicare (Medicaid) providers.

Who qualifies for Medicare benefits?

Usually, everyone age 65 and older who is eligible for Social Security benefits is also eligible for Medicare benefits. Spouses of covered eligible persons are entitled to Social Security benefits and those covered by the Railroad Retirement Act are also qualified.

If you are less than 65 years of age and have been entitled to Social Security Disability benefits for at least two years, you may be eligible for Medicare. Any person with irreversible kidney failure requiring dialysis or a transplant to maintain life can receive Medicare benefits. Also, federal retirees who became eligible for federal retirement benefits after January 1, 1991 are also entitled to Medicare benefits.

If you are not covered, you can purchase Medicare insurance. Go to your local Social Security office to ask about buying this coverage. You would receive the same Medicare coverage as a qualified Medicare recipient (see section, "Medicare Part A").

What medical expenses does Medicare cover?

Medicare is divided into two parts, *Medicare Part A* and *Medicare Part B.*

Part A is free for everyone eligible for Medicare benefits. Part B is voluntary insurance coverage for which you can choose to pay. When you enroll in Medicare, you are automatically signed up for Part B. If you don't want Part B, you must make a written request to exclude you from the coverage. If you don't make this request in writing, the cost of Part B coverage will be automatically deducted from your Social Security check. At the present time, the cost for Part B is $46.10 per month, although this amount rises each year.

Medicare Part A

Medicare Part A covers mostly hospital related claims. including hospice care, limited skilled nursing home care and some post-hospital home care. Other special services Medicare A may cover include blood transfusions and inpatient psychiatric care. Although there are high deductibles, Part A will pay most of the first 60 days in a hospital. For the period from 61 days to 90 days in a hospital, Medicare will pay any costs over the first $163 per day. A good rule of thumb as to whether Medicare will cover a specific treatment is to ask whether the treatment is medically necessary. If it is, chances are Medicare will pay at least a portion of the cost.

Medicare Part A: Hospital insurance

1. The information on this chart is accurate as of January 1995. It will change each year.
2. The benefit period begins on the first day you receive services as an inpatient in a hospital and ends after you have been out of the hospital or skilled nursing facility for 60 days in succession.
3. To the extent the blood deductible is met under one part of Medicare during a calendar year, it does not have to be met under the other part.

Nursing home care

Although nursing home care wouldn't appear to fall under Medicare guidelines, in fact, some skilled nursing homes are partially covered by Medicare. If you require 24-hour-a-day supervision and need help doing routine daily activities such as using the bathroom, taking your medicine or eating, Medicare will pay any costs over the first $87 per day, provided you meet certain criteria. You must have been hospitalized for at least three days prior to entering the nursing home.

Unfortunately, most of you will not enter a nursing home directly from a hospital. It is this requirement that places a severe burden on most people and may in fact cause you great financial hardship. For this reason, it's essential that you plan well ahead of time how you would pay for a nursing home for yourself or your spouse.

Hospice care

Hospice services which include medical social services, home health aides, counseling and therapy can be very helpful to you and your family. In order to get hospice care, you must be terminally ill with a maximum life expectancy of six

MEDICARE PART A: MEDICAL INSURANCE

Service	Medicare Benefits	Your Cost
Hospitalization	● Full cost after deductible is met (1st-60th day)	● $652 per benefit period in 1992
	● Full cost after co-insurance (61st-90th day)	● $163 per day co-insurance in 1992
	● Full cost after co-insurance for 60 lifetime reserve days, OR	● $326 per day co-insurance in 1992
	● $0 after 60 reserve days are used.	● Full cost
Post-hospital care in a certified skilled-nursing facility (SNF)	● 100% of approved amounts for the first 20 days of care each benefit period after 3-day hospital stay	● $0
	● Full cost after co-insurance (21st-100th day)	● $81.50 per day co-insurance in 1992
	● $0 after 100th day	● Full cost
Intermediate and custodial nursing care	● $0	● Full cost
Home health care	● 100% of approved amount of Medicare-approved services	● $0
	● 80% of approved amount for durable medical equipment	● 20% of approved amount in 1992
Hospice	● All but limited costs for outpatient drugs and inpatient respite care	● Limited cost-sharing for outpatient drugs and inpatient respite care
Blood	● Full cost after first 3 pints	● First 3 pints

months. However, continuing services are provided to survivors of the deceased. Your doctor or hospital can refer to you a local hospice if you need these services. Hospice services are usually covered by Medicare.

Home health care

If a doctor prescribes treatment for intermittent home health care, this service will be covered by Medicare. Medicare guidelines specify that the care be part-time and intermittent, up to six days per week for up to three consecutive weeks. Treatment cannot take more than a total of 35 hours per week.

Usually this care covers skilled nursing care, occupational therapy for people who have qualified for home health care benefits, etc.

Medicare Part B

Medicare Part B is the optional part of Medicare. This is the coverage that would pay for visits to a doctor's office. The main problem with this plan is that it has been steadily increasing in cost. In 1995, the cost was $46.10 per month (but you may be eligible for free Medicare Part B benefits—see section entitled "Are you eligible for Medicare Part B for free?").

Like Medicare Part A, everything is not simply covered. There are co-payments, deductibles, etc. If you don't have a supplement provided by your previous employer for an affordable price, you should consider getting Part B coverage. The scope of the coverage is as follows:

Medicare Part B: Medical insurance

Medicare Part B is intended to help with medical costs other than hospitalization (which is covered under Medicare Part A). These expenses can include physician and surgical services, medical supplies, diagnostic tests and durable medical equipment. But, Medicare Part B does not cover many other expenses. You still may need additional coverage to make up the difference between what both parts of Medicare don't cover.

Doctors' visits

Among the covered medical visits are: surgery, consultation, diagnostic procedures that are part of your treatment, some medical supplies, medications, physical therapy, speech therapy, speech pathology and some other services. Specialty treatments such as psychiatric visits and dental services may be covered.

Outpatient hospital services

Usually this covers services billed to the hospital such as x-rays, laboratory work or emergency services. A breakdown of costs is as follows:

MEDICARE PART B: MEDICAL INSURANCE

Service	Medicare Benefits	Your Cost
Physician and surgical services, medical supplies, diagnostic tests, durable medical equipment	● 80% of approved amounts exceeding the annual deductible of $100	● $100 each year plus 20% of approved amounts plus additional amounts charged by doctors who do not accept assignment
Laboratory services: Blood tests, biopsies, etc.	● 100% of approved amounts	● $0
Home health care	● 100% of approved amounts for Medicare-approved services (no deductible) ● 80% of approved amount for durable medical equipment (after deductible)	● $0 ● 20% of approved amount
Outpatient hospital care	● 80% of approved amount (after deductible)	● 20% of approved amount
Blood	● 80% of approved amount after first 3 pints	● First 3 pints plus 20% of approved amount for additional pints (2)

Possible other Part B covered procedures:

1. Certain drugs that cannot be self-administered.
2. X-rays and other diagnostic tests.
3. Certain types of Durable Medical Equipment (DME). Durable Medical Equipment consists of wheelchairs, special hospital beds, dialysis machines, etc.
4. Certain ambulance services to and from medical institutions or when other transportation would endanger the recipient's health.
5. Certain preventative medical procedures such as mammography screening.
6. Chiropractic care for manual manipulation of the spine only to correct subluxation as demonstrated by an x-ray.
7. Podiatric treatment for common problems such as: plantar warts, bunion deformities, ingrown toenails, etc. Most routine foot care is not covered.
8. Plastic surgery for deformities or treatments needed as a result of accidents.
9. Selected dental procedures if there is a medical necessity for such treatment.

There are many more partial hospitalization services and random coverage included in Part B benefits:

1. Occupational therapy.
2. Social workers, trained psychiatrists and psychiatric nurses, family counselors, patient training and education.
3. Help in paying for outpatient rehabilitations, under certain conditions.
4. Pap smears for early detection of cervical cancer, limited to once every three years unless you are at high risk as determined by the HCFA.
5. A pair of eyeglasses if necessary after cataract surgery.
6. Certain drugs related to HIV.

It is important you understand the little nuances of what is and is not covered.

The preceding list is not complete; it is meant to provide you with an introduction to the various rules of Medicare. The key is to have a genuine medical reason for the treatment. Here are some examples:

- Susan would like a routine physical. Would Medicare cover it? No. However, if there was a medical ailment that required a physical, Medicare probably would cover it.
- Susan has always been unhappy with the appearance of her nose. If she decided to have an operation to reduce the size of her nose,

would Medicare pay for it? No. However, if the size of Susan's nose created breathing problems that impacted her general health and several physicians agreed that a nose operation to help clear the passages and reduce the passage size (and her nose at the same time) would be medically necessary for Susan's health, the procedure probably would be covered.

Summary

Unfortunately, many people assume that on their 65th birthday Medicare will magically kick in and pay for all medical treatment. This notion is both old-fashioned and inaccurate. From this chapter, you have a working knowledge of what Medicare will cover and what is likely to be excluded from coverage. It is your job to get the most benefits you can from Medicare. This means you will have to take a proactive step to try to have as much of your treatment as possible covered. You should review this chapter carefully so that you understand exactly what is covered by both parts of Medicare. In the next chapter, you will learn what strategies are likely to help you get Medicare coverage for more of your medical treatments.

Chapter 11

Making the most of Medicare

How to file a claim

You must submit a Medicare payment form (1490). Most Medicare doctors' offices, approved carriers and Social Security offices have copies of this form. Usually, a nurse will help you complete it, but the instructions on the back are fairly clear.

For all Medicare Part B claims, the bills must be submitted by your doctor or Medicare carrier without charge.

The Medicare carriers (see appendix for list) are private insurance companies in different regions that handle the claim processing for Medicare. The carrier will withhold the $100 deductible and pay 80 percent of the remaining amount deemed "reasonable" according to Medicare definition. It will be your responsibility to pay the 20 percent difference as well as 100 percent of the amount that was charged to you in excess of the "reasonable charge."

You usually pay your doctor the 20 percent that Medicare does not pay. (Doctors are not supposed to charge you more than 20 percent but it's important that you review your doctor bills and watch out for any charges that appear to be higher than this amount). Find out if your doctor accepts *assignment*. This means that the doctor will charge Medicare no more than the approved charge. Then, you'll only be responsible for the 20 percent that Medicare does not reimburse the doctor. If your doctor doesn't accept assignment, then you must pay all charges beyond what Medicare reimburses the physician.

Before you submit a claim, you should start a log of all your medical visits and any treatment you receive. If you have accurate records of your visits and bills, then you'll know if you're being incorrectly billed. Also, having a log will be helpful if you have to file an appeal to Medicare.

If your doctor accepts assignment, he or she will usually submit the bill to Medicare on your behalf. Along with the bill, your doctor will submit form HCFA-1500, which you will need to authorize. By law, you are also required to receive an itemized bill. The *itemized bill* must show:

1. The date you received the medical procedure.
2. The place where you received the service.
3. A description of the service.
4. The charge for each specific procedure or service.
5. The provider of these services.
6. The patient's name and health insurance claim number.

It's essential you carefully review the bill; it's quite common for hospital and doctors' bills to have errors, and it's unlikely the mistakes will be in your favor. If you don't review the bill, chances are you and Medicare (which is ultimately our taxes) will overpay. You should compare the bill to the log and check which bills Medicare should be paying.

Once you have reviewed the itemized bills to find out what has already been paid, you can continue processing the claim. Here are a few suggestions to help make this process go smoothly:

1. Send copies, not original bills. Occasionally, you may be asked to send an original; if so, make sure you keep a copy for yourself.
2. When you get a bill, don't immediately pay without making certain it is a bill that you haven't already paid. You should also ask the provider whether a copy has been sent to Medicare. If a bill has not already been sent, you can also send copies of bills to the local Medicare carrier yourself (see appendix for Medicare carriers).
3. Make certain your name is legible on any document you send. Include your Medicare number on *all* pages of the bill since the pages can be separated during processing.
4. Question the amount of your bill. If your health care provider accepts Medicare assignment you should not pay more than the 20 percent. Generally, you will be notified ahead of time if Medicare will not cover a particular treatment. If you can prove you were not notified, you may not have to pay the bill. Also, don't be surprised if bills come in months after treatment or for wildly inaccurate amounts. If you feel that there is a mistake with your bill, contact the doctor or provider. If necessary, review your bills with someone experienced in Medicare claims (contact your local Area for the Aging for a counselor.)

5. Keep careful records of treatments, bills and when payment was made by Medicare. The more organized you are, the better prepared you'll be if you have to file an appeal.

How long should you wait before contacting Medicare to check on the status of a claim?

It usually takes from 35 to 45 days for a claim to be paid. If you have not received a check or a document from Medicare called *Explanation of Your Medicare Part B Benefits* after 45 days, contact the Medicare carrier for your region (the names of the Medicare carriers for your region are in the appendix).

What Medicare doesn't cover: How to read between the lines and maximize your benefits

What if you can't afford the steep deductibles that are imposed by Medicare? What if you need oral surgery or foot care? If you need to spend time in a long-term care facility, who will pay?

Costs such as these can quickly add up to hundreds of thousands of dollars. If you don't plan how you will pay for these expenses, you could find yourself in dire financial straits. It's essential you create a financial plan so that you're not caught by surprise if you incur any of these expenses. Create a plan and don't let these costs catch you by surprise.

Medicare does not cover many of the medical expenses you'll have. Obviously, it doesn't cover your deductibles for doctors' visits and hospital stays. In general, Medicare does not cover preventative medicine. It's unfortunate, but even if you're trying to stay healthy and save Medicare money in the long run, Medicare probably won't cover these measures. Some reminders:

1. You have to pay 20 percent of the approved charges and there may be additional nonapproved charges as well.
2. Many dental, eye, prescription and other health services are not covered. In addition, routine services such as hearing aids, routine physicals, immunization vaccines, orthopedic shoes, cosmetic surgery are not usually covered. You can get a complete list of coverage from the Social Security Administration.

Remember, if you want Medicare to cover a doctor's visit, there has to be a reason for your visit. Say your doctor gives you a physical exam. Generally, this wouldn't be covered by Medicare. However, if you have told your doctor that you're having dizzy spells or can't stop shaking, then your exam will probably be covered by Medicare.

One problem with this approach is that your "ailment" goes into your medical file. If you subsequently try to obtain other insurance such as life insurance, long-term care, etc., your records will be reviewed by the insurer.

Medicare rarely pays for any type of nursing-home stay. Although Medicare is supposed to pay for a certain amount of "skilled" nursing care, there are many caveats and restrictions. In addition, most people in nursing homes are not in "skilled" facilities. It's estimated that Medicare only pays approximately 2 percent of all claims for nursing homes.

If you are worried about how you'll be able to pay for whatever Medicare doesn't cover, you should consider a Medicare supplement (see Chapter 12). You should also learn how to use asset protection techniques so that you don't spend all of your money on a catastrophic illness (for more advice on this topic, read my book, *Safeguard Your Hard-Earned Savings*).

Appealing a Medicare decision

Because of the cost containment measures imposed on Medicare that have led to many benefits being cut, it's likely that any procedure not specifically addressed by Medicare regulations will be rejected. When you appeal a decision, it may be obvious that Medicare should have covered the treatment if it was medically necessary. Again, however, you have the burden to prove this by filing an appeal.

You shouldn't hesitate to file an appeal, but you should prepare yourself for a time consuming appeals process. Have all your bills and other notes handy. Find out what procedures have been paid for and what have not. Keep notes from your doctor advising you that a particular treatment would be covered.

Once you have learned that your claim was denied, ask for a review from the Medicare carrier that handled the claim. On the notice of denial are instructions on how to ask for a review. You have six months from receipt of the denial in which to appeal.

If you're still dissatisfied after you receive a written explanation of the review, and the amount in dispute is at least $100, you can request a hearing before a carrier hearing officer. You'll receive a hearing date and the right to present your case.

After the hearing with the carrier officer, if you are still dissatisfied with the outcome and the amount you are disputing is at least $500, you can request a hearing before an administrative law judge. You must make this request within 60 days of the outcome of the hearing with the carrier officer.

If you're a member of an HMO or another Medicare supplement organization, you can also appeal a decision made by the HMO. When you sign up to become a member of an HMO, you will get a packet of information which will include details on the appeals process. If you don't have this information, ask the HMO to send it to you.

The appeals process can be difficult and help is available if you need it. Some social service agencies will provide help and other groups will help you complete the required forms (look in Chapter 14 under "Medicare help agencies").

What are Peer Review Organizations (PROs)?

Peer Review Organizations are groups of doctors and other health care professionals who are paid by the federal government to review the care given to Medicare patients.

PROs operate independently in each state and are designed to evaluate whether the care is reasonable, necessary and provided in the most appropriate setting. This appraisal will determine whether Medicare should pay and what amounts should be paid. PROs have the power to deny a claim if not medically necessary. PROs can investigate individual customer complaints. (See appendix for the PRO listed for your state.) If you feel you were not given the quality of care you were entitled to, you should contact your local PRO.

Approved Charges

It is vital that you understand what is meant by Approved Charges, also known as Recognized or Allowable Charges. If a doctor charges you $200 and the Medicare-Approved Charge for that service is $100, you may have to pay $20 for the first deductible that Medicare covers (20 percent of $100) and then 100 percent of the additional $100. You would end up paying $120 for the $200 service.

In January, 1992, the Health Care Financing Administration (HCFA) started a five-year phase-in system to evaluate these charges. Every January, the HCFA establishes fee schedules which physicians must follow for the services covered by Medicare. However, there is still room for interpretation because the formula for a "reasonable" fee schedule is complicated.

Put simply, the physician's fee is determined by a formula which uses a relative value. For example, one doctor has an established practice in Los Angeles for the last 10 years and has worked exclusively in one specialty. Another doctor is new at practicing medicine, works in a rural Michigan town and doesn't specialize in this particular field of medicine. The doctor in Los Angeles is going to be allowed a higher allowance by Medicare than the doctor in Michigan because of these factors. This is what is meant by relative value.

Under this new system, Medicare payments will rise dramatically for primary care and cognitive services, but will probably decline for procedure-based services. The payments for the family and general practitioners will also increase significantly. However, payments for surgical specialties will decrease. The new system will favor primary care in most rural areas. Conversely, the system will be penalizing specialized procedures and urban areas. The new fee schedules and rules must be completely phased in by 1996.

Even with the new system addressing the fee issues, there will still be disputes and discrepancies regarding coverage and amount of payment. Doctors can still charge more than the Approved Charge. And, if your supplement does not pay this charge, you are required to pay it. That's another reason why you should learn how to dispute a ruling if you feel that you have been incorrectly charged for a service.

Ask your doctor if he or she accepts *assignment*. As explained in the section, "How to file a claim," a doctor who accepts assignment has agreed not to charge over what Medicare has deemed an approved or reasonable charge.

Are you eligible for Medicare benefits for free?

Certain programs are in place that will pay for Medicare Part B benefits for qualified people.

Qualified Medicare Beneficiary (QMB) program

For this program, you must:

1. Be eligible for Medicare Part A.
2. Have monthly income at or below the federal poverty level (not including a monthly $20 exclusion which is not counted).
3. Have personal assets not more than double the value of SSI benefits (see SSI section). In 1994 this number was $4,000 for individuals and $6,000 for couples.

If these three factors apply to you, then you should qualify for QMB. This program will also pay many of the Medicare co-payments and deductibles that you have to pay, as well as the cost of the Part B insurance and Part B co-payments and deductibles.

Specified Low-Income Medicare Beneficiaries program

Another program called "Specified Low-Income Medicare Beneficiaries" (SLMB) is open to people whose monthly income is no more than 120 percent of the federal poverty level in 1995. These people receive free Medicare Part B.

Blind and disabled Medicare recipients can usually receive Medicare Part B free of charge.

To find out if you are eligible for these programs and how to participate, you should contact the local Social Security or Medicaid office (also called Department of Social Services). A local Area for the Aging group may provide some help, as well.

How does Medicare pay the hospital that you use?

The average length of stay in a hospital for adults over age 65 is roughly nine days. That's a relatively short period of time considering the problems elderly patients can have. However, again, because of cost containment measures imposed on Medicare, generally as soon as you are stabilized, Medicare coverage will stop and you will be expected to leave the hospital.

Hospitals are paid based on a system called *Diagnostic Related Groups (DRG)*. The hospital will be paid a specific amount of money by Medicare, *regardless of the length of hospital stay*, based on what medical illness or diagnosis you have.

For example, you are admitted to the hospital for a heart bypass. This is placed in a DRG and the hospital is paid a fixed amount of money regardless of the length of stay.

Many people view this system as completely fair and just. On the other hand, the hospital makes money if you're discharged sooner than the average length of stay for your particular diagnosis. Conversely, the hospital loses money if you have to stay longer. Since the hospital is being paid a fixed amount of money regardless of how many days you're there, you could argue there's a financial incentive for the hospital to discharge you early.

Furthermore, unless the patient protests being discharged, the attending physician will recommend a discharge, usually the hospital will approve it and the patient will be discharged. Some opponents of the system say the doctors are under hospital-imposed pressure to discharge their patients early.

It's very frustrating because it seems as if you can still be seriously ill but forced to leave the hospital very quickly. And, there's not much you can do about it. The best advice is to know and trust your primary care physician so that you can feel comfortable with his or her decisions about your care.

Now that you're aware of how the hospital system works in conjunction with Medicare, you should feel ready to fight back if necessary. If you feel that you're not ready to be discharged, go through the proper channels to present your case. The following advice should help you through this process:

1. Ask your doctor or a hospital administrator for a written explanation as to why certain actions are being taken on your behalf. The specific form you need is the *Notice of Noncoverage.*

2. Talk directly with your doctor. Usually the doctor makes the decision to release a patient. Sometimes, a hospital official reviews the discharge. The Peer Review Organization (PRO) is supposed to periodically review these discharge procedures.

   If a patient does not disagree with a discharge, often nothing happens. Your doctor should keep in contact with you and help decide your course of treatment. If your doctor agrees with the Notice of Non-Coverage and thinks you should be discharged, you should find out the position of the PRO representative. If your doctor and the PRO representative agree, a PRO will review your case if you request it. If the PRO and the doctor disagree, that the hospital will request that the PRO reviews the physician's decision.

3. If you do not ask for the Notice of Non-Coverage and a review by a PRO, you will be billed for any time that you stay in a hospital, three days after receiving the Notice of Non-Coverage.

If you receive Medicare assistance, could you be discharged by a hospital?

The rules are confusing but you cannot be discharged for medical cost reasons. You can only be discharged if you are medically ready. You also have the right to be kept informed of any decisions made on your behalf regarding your medical care.

Will Medicare cover you if you get sick outside the United States?

Generally, Medicare does not pay for medical services or hospitalization while you're outside the United States. However, there are exceptions, particularly if you're in Canada and Mexico. Generally, Medicare will cover the following situations.

1. If you are in the United States and an emergency occurs in which you need immediate care, you can use a Canadian or Mexican hospital if it is closer than the nearest United States hospital.

2. If you are traveling in Canada or coming from Alaska to one of the other 48 states, you can get emergency care at a Canadian hospital.

3. If you live in the United States and need medical care (even if it is not an emergency) and a Canadian or Mexican hospital where you could get treatment is much closer than the nearest United States hospital, you can go to a hospital in Mexico or Canada.

Summary

This chapter has detailed the coverage available under Medicare. Some of the program benefits are quite helpful, such as the free Part B insurance for certain individuals. However, the system has some major drawbacks as well and the amount of coverage is likely to be reduced because of the government's efforts to cut programs such as Medicare. Still, you should take full advantage of all the benefits available to you. To do so, you have to be your own advocate. Don't rely on your doctor or hospital to keep accurate records or provide correct bills. By tracking your hospital visits, charges and payments to the providers, you'll be able to make certain that you're getting all the benefits you should.

Understand how the system works. Learn what an Approved Charge is. Ask your doctor or an elder care counselor how you can get treatment covered. Be assertive: challenge bills if you think you've been overcharged. File an appeal with Medicare if you think you've been unjustly denied benefits. Medicare isn't a perfect system, but given the alternative of using up all your savings to pay medical expenses, it's important that you learn to make the most of it.

Chapter 12

Medicare supplements, HMOs and private insurance

Medicare supplements

Medicare supplements are supplemental insurance policies designed to pay for things Medicare does not cover. These policies can be quite helpful because Medicare pays for far less than what you might expect.

There are many types of supplements being sold in the United States today. In the past, there were many unscrupulous sales practices involving these policies, and the policies themselves were often confusing. To address these problems, the Medigap Fraud and Abuse Prevention Act of 1990 made several significant changes regarding the sale of Medicare supplemental insurance policies.

Among the changes under the new rules which became effective since the passage of the 1992 Federal Act:

1. It is illegal for an insurance company or salesperson to transfer you to another policy which significantly duplicates your current Medicare supplemental policy. In fact, if a sales person recommends that you switch from your existing policy, the sales person is required to provide you with a form that states why your old policy is being surrendered. You are required to sign this form.

2. People who are eligible for *Medicaid* cannot be sold a Medicare insurance policy. Some sales people will try to coerce you into buying a policy that isn't necessary. If you're already on Medicaid, many of your expenses will be covered. Agents are required to ask individuals if they are currently on Medicaid. Agents who sell a policy to a Medicaid recipient are subject to fines. Don't fall prey to an unscrupulous agent who insists that you need a policy—if you are on Medicaid, you do not need a supplement.

3. All Medigap policies are *guaranteed renewable*. Once you have this insurance coverage, regardless of the state of your health, your coverage cannot be canceled unless you stop paying the premium.

4. You shouldn't be denied coverage, provided you apply at the correct time. The rule states that you cannot be denied coverage *for any reason* if you get your policy within six months of becoming eligible for Medicare. After this time period, one six-month waiting period for preexisting conditions can be required, but your medical history cannot be used to determine how much your premiums will be. If you find a reason to switch to a new policy, once your original one has been in effect for six months, your new insurer cannot require a waiting period.

5. Premiums cannot be increased without a plan. A plan means that the insurance company cannot simply raise your premium because you get older or often take ill. In order to raise your premium, the insurance company must get approval (usually from the state insurance commissioner) and the rates must be raised uniformly for everyone in a particular category of insurance. States are required to have a process for approving insurance companies' requests for premium increases. A public hearing is held so that consumers can learn about proposed increases and give their comments.

6. Many states have adopted a special type of Medigap policy called a *Coordinated Care Medigap Policy*. This policy is offered under the new *Medicare Select Program* and features lower premiums for Medicare recipients. The premiums are kept low because the Medicare beneficiary must receive medical care only from doctors selected by the insurance company.

   Currently Medicare Select is available in Alabama, Arizona, California, Florida, Illinois, Indiana, Kentucky, Massachusetts, Michigan, Minnesota, Missouri, North Dakota, Ohio, Oregon, Texas, Washington and Wisconsin.

7. Counseling is available if you need additional help comparing policies or understanding particular clauses in your coverage. (See the appendix for a state-by-state directory of insurance offices. The toll-free Medicare hotline number is 1-800-638-6833).

Medicare supplement policies

Medicare supplement polices (Medigap) are now standardized in 10 basic plans, identified by the letters A through J.

When you look for a Medicare supplement, you should consider the factors that are important to you. Do you want a supplement that will pay for preventative health care such as routine physicals or is prescription drug coverage more important? Or, are both these factors significant?

Not every state has all 10 options available. The basic policy, Plan A, must be made available to Medicare recipients everywhere.

What to look for in a Medicare supplement

Coverage

You should know exactly what you are buying. A good policy will pay all the co-insurance amounts. For example, if Medicare pays 80 percent and you pay 20 percent, the supplement should pay the 20 percent. If a doctor charges you over and above the Medicare Approved Charge, the supplement should pay that extra amount. Ideally, the supplement pays for items not covered by Medicare. For example, if Medicare will only pay for part-time, intermittent home health care for up to three weeks, the supplement should pay for care up to six weeks.

Quality of carrier

The quality of the carrier is one of the most important considerations in choosing a Medicare supplement. You should know how the insurance company is rated: The AAA rating by Standard and Poor's is the highest rating available. The ratings show the stability of the company and the likelihood that the insurer will be in business for many years to come. You want a company that has a good reputation in the Medicare supplement field. You want an insurer that pays most claims and pays them promptly. You should ask a prospective insurance company what percentage of claims they pay. Obviously, 100 percent is unrealistic, but the higher the rate, the better off you'll be.

You may even want to visit a library and do some research, reading articles about the insurer you're considering. These articles should give you a more objective perspective about the insurance company. Obviously, if there has been a good deal of negative press about the insurer, you may want to select another company.

Type of filing

You know how difficult filing Medicare claims can be. Some insurance companies with Medicare supplements have electronic filing systems, so the doctor's office processes your claims electronically. This added benefit reduces the hassles of claim filing and could save you hours of tracking, making initial payments, etc.

You shouldn't choose a supplemental policy simply because it has electronic filing but if you're considering one or two policies that are very similar, consider the convenience factor of electronic filing.

Accessibility

You also want an insurer that has an effective customer service department available to handle your questions. A toll-free number is always a plus. You can even call the home office to ask a question before you buy the insurance. See how long you're put on hold or whether you're transferred to several operators before you get help. How you'll be treated on the phone is often a good clue to the type of service the insurer will provide.

In addition, you should ask your doctors if they're familiar with the company you're selecting. Ask whether they've heard of the insurer or if they've had any problems with the company. The last thing you want is to make life harder, instead of easier, when you buy a supplement. If your doctor has had trouble dealing with the company, think twice before getting a policy from that insurer.

Cost

The old saying, "If you buy a diamond for a dime, it is probably worth a dime," applies to supplement policies. You may find two seemingly identical policies with an almost 50 percent difference in price. Obviously, the policies don't include the same coverage. Since the costs for Medicare supplements can be steep, you should comparison shop quite carefully. Among considerations for cost are:

- Will the premiums rise as you get older? How much will they increase? Some premiums are set at the age when you buy the policy. Meaning, if you buy a policy at age 65, you will always pay the rate that the company charges people who are 65, no matter what your current age is. On the other hand, if the premium is based on *attained age*, then the costs will go up every year as you get older. The appeal of attained age policies is that the premium is often quite low when you're younger. Finally, some carriers charge the same, regardless of age.

- Can the premium rise with inflation or sickness? You want the least expensive premium for all the coverage you need. You have to decide whether you can afford the policy today as well as in the future.

- Ask about the insurer's policy on preexisting conditions. For example, if you had back surgery, will the new policy exclude any coverage for your back? If it does, for how long is the coverage excluded?

Try to narrow down your search to three insurance companies, without taking cost into account. Call the three carriers and ask for a "specimen policy." Read each one word for word. Don't take any seemingly irrelevant phrases, such as

"Approved Charges," for granted. Reviewing every word of the policy will provide you with a better grasp of the policy's coverage.

Supplements can provide excellent benefits, but the policies are often expensive and confusing. Do your research well before your 65th birthday so you don't feel rushed to make a decision without understanding what policy you're buying.

Standard Medigap plans

Following is a list of the 10 standard plans and the benefits provided by each:

Description of Medigap insurance Plans A-J

Plan A (the basic policy) consists of these core benefits:

- Coverage for the Part A co-insurance amount ($169 per day in 1993) for the 61st day through the 90th day of hospitalization in each Medicare benefit period.

- Coverage for the Part A co-insurance amount ($338 per day in 1993) for each of Medicare's 60 nonrenewable lifetime hospital in-patient reserve days used.

- After all Medicare hospital benefits are exhausted, coverage for 100 percent of the Medicare Part A eligible hospital expenses. Coverage is limited to a maximum of 365 days of additional inpatient hospital care during the policyholder's lifetime. This benefit is paid either at the rate Medicare pays hospitals under its Prospective Payment System or another appropriate standard of payment.

- Coverage under Medicare Parts A and B for the reasonable cost of the first three pints of blood, or equivalent quantities of packed red blood cells per calendar year unless replaced in accordance with federal regulations.

- Coverage for the co-insurance amount for Part B series (generally 20 percent of approved amount) after the $100 annual deductible is met.

Plan B includes core benefits plus:

- Coverage for the Medicare Part A inpatient hospital deductible ($676 per benefit period in 1993).

Plan C includes core benefits plus:

- Coverage for the Medicare Part A deductible.
- Coverage for skilled nursing facility care co-insurance amount ($84.50 per days for days 21 through 100 per benefit period in 1993).
- Coverage for the Medicare Part B deductible ($100 per calendar year in 1993).
- Coverage for medically necessary emergency care in a foreign country.

Plan D includes core benefits plus:

- Coverage for the Medicare Part A deductible.
- Coverage for the skilled nursing facility care daily co-insurance amount.
- Coverage for medically necessary emergency care in a foreign country.
- Coverage for at-home recovery. The at-home recovery benefit pays up to $1,600 per year for short-term, at-home assistance with activities of daily living (bathing, dressing, personal hygiene, etc.) for those recovering from an illness, injury or surgery. There are various benefit requirements and limitations.

Plan E includes core benefits plus:

- Coverage for the Medicare Part A deductible.
- Coverage for the skilled nursing facility care daily co-insurance amount.
- Coverage for medically necessary emergency care in a foreign country.
- Coverage for preventive medical care. The preventive medical care benefit pays up to $120 per year for examinations including a physical, flu shot, serum cholesterol screening, hearing test, diabetes screening and thyroid function test.

Plan F includes core benefits plus:

- Coverage for the Medicare Part A deductible.
- Coverage for the skilled nursing facility care daily co-insurance amount.
- Coverage for the Medicare Part B deductible.
- Coverage for medically necessary emergency care in a foreign country.
- Coverage for 100 percent of Medicare Part B excess charges.*

Plan G includes core benefits plus:

- Coverage for the Medicare Part A deductible.
- Coverage for the skilled nursing facility care daily co-insurance amount.
- Coverage for 80 percent of Medicare Part B excess charges.*
- Coverage for medically necessary emergency care in a foreign country.
- Coverage for at-home recovery (see Plan D).

Plan H includes core benefits plus:

- Coverage for the Medicare Part A deductible.
- Coverage for the skilled nursing facility care daily co-insurance amount.
- Coverage for medically necessary emergency care in a foreign country.

- Coverage for 50 percent of the cost of prescription drugs up to a maximum annual benefit of $1,250 after the policyholder meets a $250 per year deductible. (This is called the "basic" prescription drug benefit.)

Plan I includes core benefits plus:

- Coverage for the Medicare Part A deductible.
- Coverage for the skilled nursing facility care daily co-insurance amount.
- Coverage for 100 percent of Medicare Part B excess charges.*
- Basic prescription drug coverage (see Plan H for description).
- Coverage for medically necessary emergency care in a foreign country.
- Coverage for at-home recovery (see Plan D).

Plan J includes core benefits plus:

- Coverage for the Medicare Part A deductible.
- Coverage for the skilled nursing facility care daily co-insurance amount.
- Coverage for Medicare Part B deductible.
- Coverage for 100 percent Medicare Part B excess charges.*
- Coverage for medically necessary emergency care in a foreign country.
- Coverage for preventive medical care (see Plan E).
- Coverage for at-home recovery (see Plan D).
- Coverage for 50 percent of the cost of prescription drugs up to a maximum annual benefit of $3,000 after the policyholder meets a $250 per year deductible. (This is called the "extended" prescription drug benefit.)

*Plan pays a specified percentage of the difference between the Medicare's approved amount or Part B services and the actual charges (up to the amount of charge limitations set by either Medicare or state law).

Medicare Select

This is a newer program currently available in 15 states with more states expected to make it available over the next two years. Medicare Select is like a Medicare supplement but usually pays Medigap benefits only for items and services provided by specified health care professionals and facilities. If you use other doctors or other hospitals, the policy may pay only partial benefits. Many of the same insurance companies and HMOs that provide standard Medigap policies will provide the select policies as well.

BENEFIT OPTIONS	Packages									
	A	B	C	D	E	F	G	H	I	J
Basic Benefits	X	X	X	X	X	X	X	X	X	X
SNF Coinsurance			X	X	X	X	X	X	X	X
Part A Deductible		X	X	X	X	X	X	X	X	X
Part B Deductible			X			X				X
Part B Excess Charges-100%						X			X	X
Part B Excess Charges-80%							X			
Foreign Travel			X	X	X	X	X	X	X	X
At-home Recovery				X			X			X
Basic Drugs ($1,250 limit)								X	X	
Extended Drugs ($3,000 limit)										X
Preventive Care					X					X

The reason to get a Select policy is to save on your premium costs. Depending on where you live, you will generally save about 30 percent compared to a regular Medigap policy.

Select policies are available in: Alabama, Arizona, California, Florida, Illinois, Indiana, Kentucky, Massachusetts, Michigan, Minnesota, Missouri, North Dakota, Ohio, Oregon, Texas, Washington and Wisconsin.

Health Maintenance Organizations (HMOs)

Medicare supplements can be too costly for many people. An alternative is to use an HMO. While you will save on your medical expenses, there are some disadvantages to an HMO. Generally, you do not get to choose your own doctors and often see a different physician from one visit to the next.

If you're comfortable seeing different doctors and need to save money, then HMOs are viable options. You should choose an HMO carefully since the services vary a great deal. You should follow the same evaluation you would for supplement policies. Find out all relevant details on the costs, how often they will increase and whether prescriptions are covered. You should also find out whether the doctors in the HMO have one central office or if you visit the doctors wherever they're located. Obviously, if the doctors aren't easily accessible, you may want to select another HMO. You should also find out the HMO's policy on second opinions. Some HMOs discourage second opinions, although you will probably want to get one if you need any major surgery.

One of the best ways to evaluate the service at an HMO is to ask friends who use an HMO what they think. Ask about their experience with a particular HMO. Find out how long patients generally have to wait, whether the staff is friendly and helpful, whether the costs have been reasonable, etc.

Regardless of whether you use a private Medicare supplement or HMO, you will still not be covered for every contingency. One of the biggest costs facing mature Americans and one of the hardest decisions to accept is that you may well need custodial care (for more information, refer to my book *Safeguard Your Hard-Earned Savings*).

What if you disagree with the service you get at the HMO?

Just as you disputed Medicare service, you can dispute your care at an HMO. First, ask for a reconsideration within 60 days after you receive the Notice of Initial Determination. Your request must be made in writing to your HMO or local Social Security office. Keep a copy for your records and get a receipt if you hand deliver it or send it by certified mail.

If the HMO does not rule in your favor, it is required to send your reconsideration request to the Health Care Financing Administration for a review and determination.

Nursing homes

The sheer number of people using some type of assisted living is astronomical. It's distressing how easily a stay in a nursing home could turn a wealthy man into a pauper. Usually even the best of Medicare supplements or HMOs don't cover more than 100 days in a nursing home. Also, the policies often have so many restrictions that you end up having to pay out of your pocket for your stay.

There are three types of nursing homes used most often. These are skilled care, intermediate care and custodial care.

Skilled care

This includes 24-hour-a-day supervision. A registered nurse is always on duty to administer prescription drugs or to help with all other tasks such as bathing, eating or using the bathroom. Ironically, this is the care that is least used—only about .5 percent—but the best covered by Medicare. This type of care would be for seniors with major incapacitating ailments such as severe strokes.

Intermediate care

This type of care is for patients who don't require 24-hour supervision. There may still be an RN available. If someone has had a serious stroke or is confined to a wheelchair, for example, but does not need a 24-hour-a-day registered nurse but needs more supervision than a custodial care facility, this person would go into an intermediate care facility. Approximately 4.5 percent of seniors use this care.

Custodial care

This care is commonly used by seniors recovering from surgery, in the early stages of Alzheimer's or who cannot take care of themselves alone. Patients getting custodial care get help with all routine daily activities. This is the care that is most used by seniors—almost 96 percent—but is rarely covered by Medicare.

The costs of nursing homes are usually more than $150 per day, not including prescriptions or incidentals. That's why roughly half of the people who enter a nursing home face impoverishment within 13 weeks. According to the special Senate Committee on Aging, of the average person's health care costs, $.81 of every dollar pays for long-term care and $.19 for pays for care that is covered under Medicare. This is such a serious issue that it may be difficult for you to even consider this possibility.

There's no way to escape the high costs of long-term care but you should know about the strategies to get some help paying the costs. The three most likely options are: a nursing home insurance plan; converting your current life insurance into a special policy that will pay for a nursing home stay or finding a way for Medicaid to pay.

Using a long-term care insurance policy

There has been so much confusion about nursing home insurance that some elder care advisers have discouraged seniors from getting it. You should consider getting it, but compare policies very carefully and get the coverage well before you need it. If you're about to enter a nursing home, you'll have too much else to worry about to make a well thought-out decision about nursing home insurance.

Nursing home policies are not that expensive, until you reach your mid to late 60s. Long-term care insurance can usually be purchased by someone as young as 50 years of age; insurance companies usually don't offer it to people any younger. The premiums go up gradually from there. At age 60, they begin to rise and after age 65, they begin going up more dramatically. Many experts say the best time to buy this insurance is as soon as possible. This makes sense because if you wait until you need the coverage, you won't be able to buy it. Because of the cost, you should look at coverage between your 55th and 60th birthdays. If you wait until you reach age 65, you could spend 30 percent or more in higher premiums. If you wait until after you reach age 65, the premium costs will just continue to increase. Remember, your health plays an important factor in the cost of the insurance and if your health is poor, you may not even be able to get the coverage.

Benefits that should be included in a long-term health care insurance policy:

1. Make sure the insurance will pay the costs of an average stay in a nursing home.
2. The coverage should have an inflation rider since the chances are great that you won't enter a care facility until many years after you buy the policy.
3. Make sure the coverage includes payments to any type of care facility including skilled, intermediate and custodial.
4. Make sure you are not required to go directly from a hospital to a nursing home and you don't need a doctor's prescription to enter a nursing home. Check if you can be admitted for both physical and mental conditions such as dementia and Alzheimer's disease.
5. See whether the policy has any limitations on carrying another policy for home health care insurance.
6. Look for coverage that starts paying the first day you enter the nursing home since most people do not have very long stays in convalescent facilities. Also, find out whether the coverage pays for a set number of years or until you die.
7. Make sure your premium payments cease within a reasonable time—immediately to 30 days or three months after you enter the care facility.

8. Find out if there is a preexisting condition clause. For example, if you had a back operation two years prior to buying the nursing home insurance, will the policy cover you for a nursing home stay after another back operation?

9. When and how much will your premium rise? You should look for a policy with premiums that don't go up as you get older or when you enter a nursing home.

Once you understand the policies' coverage on these points, you can then compare the different policies. See how the prices and the coverage differ. Call the companies you are interested in to see how easy it is to get through and if the operators or agents are courteous and helpful. You should also find out what percentage of claims the insurer pays and what is the company's rating. The rating is particularly important since you will be relying on the coverage for years in the future and want the company to be around. Also ask about the history of premium increases for the past five years. This information will give you a sense of how your costs will go up in the future.

Don't be lazy and simply take the first policy you review. This insurance is significant and costly so you must do all the research and comparison shopping before selecting a policy.

Converting a current life insurance policy to pay for nursing home costs

With the number of people using nursing home care rising dramatically and the costs increasing just as dramatically, many insurance companies have devised a creative solution. You can convert your existing life insurance policies to special policies that will pay the cost of nursing home care when you need it.

This strategy works as follows: Your old life insurance policies have a certain amount of cash value. If you and your beneficiaries don't need the death benefit, you can have the cash value transferred through a tax-free exchange into a new insurance policy that is designed to pay a certain percentage of the death benefit to a nursing home. If you don't enter a nursing home, the death benefit goes to your spouse or beneficiaries as specified in your original life insurance policy.

While this strategy may sound straightforward, you shouldn't automatically assume it's the right answer for you. There may be limitations in your policy about nursing home coverage or the death benefit may be greatly reduced. You should compare the cost of a standard nursing home policy with what it would cost to convert the life insurance policy. Buying a straight, long-term care policy may be cheaper then rolling over your life insurance into a long-term care policy. If you're having trouble doing the calculations, consult an elder care counselor.

Summary

A high quality Medicare supplement is an extremely important part of your overall financial and estate plans. The ever increasing medical care costs make it essential you plan well ahead of the time when you will need this coverage. Remember, though, that not everyone needs a Medicare supplement. If you qualify for Medicaid, you should not get a supplement, regardless of what an insurance agent may tell you.

Assuming that you want to get a Medicare supplement, you should select a policy carefully. There are a wide range of policies at varying costs. Do your homework: Learn how the various supplemental plans work. Compare HMO coverage with the coverage of a supplemental plan. Most importantly, be absolutely clear about what the policy does and does not cover. After all, you don't want to find out later, when you need the coverage, that your policy doesn't cover what you thought it would. By selecting the right Medicare supplement, you'll be able to keep some of your savings for other purposes during your retirement years.

Chapter 13

Medicaid

Your last option for help in paying for a nursing home stay is Medicaid. The good news is Medicaid will pay for a nursing home stay if you qualify. The bad news is that you essentially have to be broke in order to qualify.

The sad reality that Medicaid is not widely available to cover nursing home expenses is quite frustrating for seniors. After all, you paid into the system with your tax dollars and have come to expect to get some benefits back when you need them. You will have coverage if you need immediate hospitalization when you break a limb or have a heart attack. However, if you have a stroke and need a place to rehabilitate, or develop Alzheimer's and need full-time care in a facility, you're basically on your own. These illnesses require you to enter a catastrophic care facility and Medicaid rarely covers these facilities, unless you've exhausted all your financial resources. When you're destitute, Medicaid will help.

You have to accept the depressing reality that you may very well end up in a long-term care facility. Don't think it only happens to someone else. Half of all seniors will require some type of long-term care. Assume that it may well happen to you, so you should plan well ahead of time to protect your assets for your spouse and other survivors. You can't afford *not* to deal with this issue.

For more tips on protecting your assets, read my book, *Safeguard Your Hard-Earned Savings*.

What is Medicaid?

Medicaid is a federal and state funded health insurance program for people who need financial aid for medical purposes. If you're in a Medicaid approved facility and you qualified for Medicaid, certain expenses for medical care would be paid. The names of the program and the requirements vary from state to state; for example, in California, Medicaid is called MediCal.

How to qualify for Medicaid

This is the tricky part. Technically, to qualify for Medicaid, you must be impoverished. In 1989 the Spousal Impoverishment Act was passed. This federal act set the guidelines that limit the total income and assets of Medicaid recipients in care facilities as well as the assets and income of their spouses.

The act established a range of assets which the states used as guidelines to set their own income and asset limits. Limits range by states; assets could range as low as $14,532 to $72,600. There are two key factors used to determine whether you qualify for Medicaid—household income and assets.

Income test

States can either be *income cap states* or *benefit states*. Most are income cap, which means that you cannot receive Medicaid for any reason if your income is over the set limit. A benefit state has the same guidelines with one major exception: If your income exceeds the limit but is less than the average cost of nursing homes in your area, you may still qualify for Medicaid.

In 1994, most states capped the well spouse's income for Medicaid eligibility at approximately $1,266 per month, although some states allowed as much as $1,720 per month. There is an index for inflation each year so these numbers rise annually.

If you live in a benefit state, you can usually petition to be allowed income over the set limit for viable reasons. Among the reasons you may have for making this petition are having a high mortgage or higher long-term care costs.

Plan ahead to keep your income below the limit

Since you don't want to go bankrupt using up all your resources to pay for nursing home coverage, try to keep your income below the Medicaid guidelines in order to qualify for Medicaid. Tactics you should consider:

1. Take your Social Security benefits at age 62 in order to get a lower monthly payment.
2. When you retire, take a lump sum payment of your pension rather than a guaranteed income option.
3. Choose investment options that have no income or let you control the amount of income you receive.
4. Move to a benefit state where the nursing home costs exceed your income.
5. Use "income only trusts" if you live in an income cap state.

The second test you must pass to qualify for Medicaid is the asset test.

Asset test

The Spousal Impoverishment Act of 1989 changed virtually all the asset guidelines. Again, the limits vary by state but generally are as follows: The minimum assets allowed are generally up to $14,532 with a maximum of $72,600 (based on 1994 numbers). These amounts increase each year.

Keep your assets to the limit of $72,600. You want anything more than this to be counted as exempt, so you will not be disqualified.

Exempt assets

An exempt asset is one that Medicaid does not include into the amount of assets Medicaid recipients are permitted to have. Examples of exempt assets include:

Your personal residence

A married couple owning a home will not have to include their residence in the Medicaid asset limitations. Most states do not stipulate the size or dollar value of the home. However, one spouse must still live in the house to use it as an exempt asset. In addition, home furnishings, home improvements and collectibles are usually exempt assets.

However, the Omnibus Reconciliation Act as amended in 1993 made the rules even stricter. Although your home may be protected during your lifetime, the federal government is encouraging states to lien homes to recoup expenses after a Medicaid recipient dies.

One car

Usually any dollar value.

Certain types of irrevocable trusts

Some irrevocable trusts that have been set up in specific ways may protect your assets. The general rule of thumb is that if you have no access to the trust and don't control the money, the contents of the trust aren't counted toward the Medicaid limit.

When you set up a trust, you, as creator of the trust, transfer an asset to another person. It is the other person's responsibility as trustee to manage and oversee the funds in the best interest of the beneficiaries. With a revocable trust, you, as creator, would probably be the trustee. Since you would have access to the funds, they would be counted toward your asset limits.

On the other hand, if you create an irrevocable trust and can't get to the assets, then Medicaid *may* not be able to get to them either. But, you need to have established the trust well before you apply for Medicaid. The duties of the trustee must have already been established and will not change if you're eligible for Medicaid.

Assume you put your assets in an irrevocable trust, naming a third party as trustee. The trust will pay the trustees $1,000 per month. This amount is fixed and cannot be changed. When your spouse dies, the trust terminates and the principal will be distributed to the beneficiaries. In theory, this type of trust would enable you to exclude assets from your Medicaid limit, but there is no absolute rule. States and even counties have been making their own decisions in this area.

You have to take into account the look-back rule which means you can't transfer any assets three years prior to applying for Medicaid. The period is five years when you transfer assets to a trust. If you're wondering whether to establish a trust, you should seek legal counsel from an elder care attorney in your community. Be wary of anyone who says you should set up a *Medicaid Qualifying Trust*. These trusts used to be very popular but they don't allow you to exclude your assets because you have too much discretion over the trust's holdings.

In summary, you need expert advice if you're setting up a trust in order to protect your assets. Remember that you don't want to have access to the principal or the income, bear in mind the look-back rules in your state and don't forget that a trust may not help you qualify for Medicaid.

Properly structured annuities and/or private pension plans

As with trusts, annuities can sometimes provide a way to protect your assets from Medicaid. Again, you have to set up the annuity in such a way that you have no control over the holdings and get no income from it. Some states have rules that annuities let you transfer assets using an unrealistic mortality assumption. Then, your annuity is essentially a gift and you would be disqualified from receiving Medicaid.

Now that you know the four general areas of protected assets, you have to decide how best to use these exemptions to protect your assets. Consider the following advice.

Pay off your home mortgage if you still have one. Since your home is protected, you should use unprotected cash to put into the house. In fact, you may even want to buy a larger home since a house of any size is protected. You should also consider making home improvements, buying new furniture or even jewelry since these assets are generally protected from the Medicaid limits.

A warning! It is becoming common for states to lien property and capture assets, *even the home*, after a Medicaid beneficiary dies. You have to consider this possibility before you do something with your home.

Buy a new car. If you are allowed one car, make sure you have a valuable new car that can be used for "medical purposes."

Utilize the proper trusts for your situation, in the proper time frame to protect your assets.

Protect your liquid cash and investments by creating private pension plans or properly structured annuities.

What you need to know about trusts

After the Omnibus Reconciliation Act was passed in 1993 (OBRA 93), the use of trusts for medical planning become severely limited. However, there are still certain trusts that can be used to protect your assets, but because OBRA 93 is so new, there is not much case law in this area. It is hard to know what position the courts or legislature will take with regard to trusts. You should talk to an attorney or other elder care expert to find out the latest rulings in this area.

Annuities for Medicaid planning

The word annuity may sound intimidating but it's not difficult to create one and a personal annuity may help protect your assets.

Assume you are considering applying for Medicaid and one spouse gets sick. At this time, you would invoke provisions already in place that you established when you created the annuity.

Your first step is the one transfer of assets that is allowed without disqualification under the 36-month look-back rule, spousal transfer. Immediately put the annuity in the healthy spouse's name if it isn't already in that name. In addition, the beneficiary must not be the sick spouse, so you should change the beneficiary to either a separate trust or other beneficiaries.

Then, you should reduce the size of the well spouse's estate so it is below the state limits. You may have to give up access to your principal by annuitizing the annuity. This means you would begin taking income for a set number of years. You should try to create an annuity that could be broken if you or your spouse dies. You also must keep the income you receive below Medicaid limits so that you're not disqualified. See if you can reduce the income by spreading it out over 30 or 40 years.

These strategies are complicated and you must discuss your options carefully with an expert. Don't use the aforementioned guidelines without seeking counsel in your community. Again, there's no guarantee that these strategies will serve to protect your assets from Medicaid. The laws can change at any time causing loopholes to close. In addition, make certain that whoever creates a plan for you uses a trustworthy custodian and look for insurance from a reputable company to protect your annuity. (For other strategies to protect your assets from Medicaid, read my book *Safeguard Your Hard-Earned Savings.*)

Additional considerations

Look-back rule

One of Medicaid's rules is the look-back rule. The rule allows Medicaid to look back on financial dealings over the last 36 months (three years). For assets in a trust (even a revocable living trust), the look-back period is extended to five years. This means that if Medicaid feels you made a transaction of gifting or giving money away, the money can be taken back. This rule doesn't apply to spousal transfers or new home purchases.

Last option: divorce

Some couples even take the drastic step of getting a divorce in order to protect their assets from Medicaid. Unfortunately, this strategy doesn't always work.. All assets are transferred to one spouse's name and then the couple gets a divorce. If you are planning to get a divorce, you will need a very convincing reason to present to the court. A judge isn't likely to grant you a divorce if your spouse of 50 years has just entered a nursing home.

Medicaid planning for an unmarried person (single or widowed)

Unfortunately, planning for a single individual is much harder, primarily because you can't take advantage of spousal transfers. Your home may not be protected and the income allowance for single people is almost nonexistent. If you have to go into a nursing home, there will be no one in your home unless you have a tenant, but having a tenant wouldn't protect a single person's home. To get around this problem these tactics are often used:

Letter of intent. You can still protect a home if you can get a doctor to sign a letter of intent stating that your stay in a nursing home is temporary and you should be able to move back to your home within six months.

Joint tenancy. You can protect your house by placing your home in joint tenancy with a child who lives in the house. Do this only if the child is living with you and you feel comfortable placing his or her name on the title with you. Be careful of going higher than the free $10,000 gift per year or you might have to pay gift taxes or use your one-time $600,000 exclusion. Remember, when you place someone's name on your asset, you are technically giving that person a gift. If the value of the gift is more than $10,000, you will be subject to gift taxes or use part or all of your $600,000 exemption. Once the property is placed in joint tenancy, you lose half of the control. If you place someone on the deed who is married, you could actually be placing two people on your property (depending on the state in which you live). You have to make sure that this transaction doesn't trigger the look-back rule as well.

Create a life estate. Suppose you as a parent sign your house deed over to the children or other beneficiaries. As long as a parent is living, the children have no rights or access to the home. Upon the parent's death, the home would go to the children. If you were to apply for Medicaid, your home would be protected and upon your death, Medicaid could not place a lien on the property because the home would not be owned by you. Unfortunately, under the new Omnibus Reconciliation

Act the use of life estates has started to be reviewed by Medicaid. You should seek legal counsel before you establish a life estate. In addition, you may not be able to take advantage of tax rules such as the step-up in tax basis that would normally apply after someone dies.

Consider annuities, gifting assets, trusts or partnerships. You can use a properly structured annuity to protect your assets. You nominate someone else as the annuitant which means he or she will receive all the income. This keeps your income below the Medicaid limits. You also have to name someone else as the beneficiary. Although you lose control of the principal while you are on Medicaid for a set number of years. This a better option because it allows you not to spend all your money on health care. Again, you should seek an attorney's advice to make sure your annuity complies with gifting, look-back and other requirements.

Summary

There's no avoiding the fact that if you live long enough, chances are you will need to spend some time in a care facility. And, more than half the occupants in long-term care facilities are on Medicaid. The sad truth is that most of these people had to spend all their savings before they could qualify for Medicaid. What's even more dismaying is that you may recover enough to leave the care facility, then have no resources to support yourself, and when you die, you will not have any savings to leave your family.

It's imperative that you learn about long-term care as well as the options available to pay for it. And, of course, you should familiarize yourself with Medicaid so that you can take full advantage of its benefits.

Chapter 14

Social Security and Medicare resources, scams and fraud

Although after reading about the difficulties of dealing with the government bureaucracies handling Medicare and other programs, you may think that you will never be able to get benefits or use these services, but you don't have to do all the work on your own. There are many agencies that will help you if you've been denied benefits or need assistance completing applications and other paperwork. Don't hesitate calling these agencies for help. Chances are if one agency can't assist you, it will be able to refer you to one that can.

Useful hotlines and contacts

The Social Security Administration

For most Social Security and Medicare questions, this should be your first stop. Either call your local office (numbers are listed in the phone book) or use the toll-free number, 800-772-1213. Hearing-impaired individuals can call a special number, 800-325-0788.

Keep in mind this is one of the busiest, if not the busiest, phone number in the United States. Don't call first thing in the morning or the first week of the month when everyone tries to get through. Call in the mid-afternoon, later in the week or later in the month.

Medicare hotline

A separate number is available for Medicare questions. The numbers are 800-234-5772 or 800-638-6833. You can ask any Medicare questions regarding insurance supplements, co-payments and how to sign up for the Medicare Qualified Beneficiary Program. You can also find out who is the local insurance carrier in your region.

Peer Review Organization

These groups are responsible for monitoring medical payments. They keep a watch on doctors to insure the physicians are following ethical standards and providing appropriate care to Medicare recipients. The PROs have the right to deny claims by individuals. (See Appendix C for a complete list of PROs per state.)

Health Care Financing Administration

If you want additional information on Medicare, Medicaid, supplements and related subjects, contact this agency.

200 Independence Avenue SW
Washington, DC 20201
800-638-6833 and 202-690-6726

Health Insurance Association of America

This industry group can answer general questions about health insurance, but not issues related to your own policies. You can contact them at 800-942-4242.

Eldercare Locator

This relatively new service is partly administered by the Area Agencies on Aging. It is designed to help you find the specific local agencies, offices and help organizations that can assist you. From this service, you can learn about Meals on Wheels, free insurance counseling, legal services, nursing homes, etc. The phone number is 800-677-1116.

Consumer Information Center

Part of the General Services Administration, this organization publishes a wide variety of pamphlets and books on Social Security, specialty entitlement programs and many other subjects.

P.O. Box 100
Pueblo, CO 81002
719-948-3334

Social Security and Medicare legal counsel for the elderly

Center for Law and Social Policy

This agency is a nonprofit, public interest law firm representing minorities, poor people and the disabled. It provides assistance in a variety of matters including child support, employment training, family law, child care and health care.

1616 P Street NW
Suite 450
Washington, DC 20036
202-328-5140
Fax: 202-328-5195

Center on Social Welfare Policy and Law

This national support center deals with issues in the cash public assistance programs such as Aid to Families with Dependent Children and Supplemental Security Income. The center will help with legal matters including referrals to local legal aid offices, private attorneys, voluntary agencies and also provide assistance to those seeking public assistance benefits.

275 Seventh Avenue
6th Fl.
New York, NY 10001
212-633-6967
Fax: 212-633-6371

1029 Vermont Avenue NW
Suite 850
Washington, DC 20005
202-347-5615
Fax: 202-347-5462

Mental Health Law Project

This project works primarily with the rights of the developmentally and mentally disabled, assisting in legal matters, strategies, counseling and training.

1101 15th Street NW
Suite 1212
Washington, DC 20005
202-467-5730
Fax: 202-223-0409

National Consumer Law Center, Inc.

This law center works as a support center representing the interest of low-income persons in consumer and energy matters. It also assists private attorneys representing eligible clients. The center publishes several publications and newsletters on consumer and energy law.

11 Beacon Street	1875 Connecticut Avenue NW
Suite 821	Washington, DC 20009
Boston, MA 02108	202-986-6060
617-523-8010	Fax: 202-986-6648

National Health Law Program

This program focuses on assisting low income clients gain better access to quality health care. It will provide litigation help, technical advice and training. This project also publishes a quarterly newsletter.

2639 South La Cienega Boulevard	1815 H Street NW
Los Angeles, CA 90034	Suite 700
310-204-6010	Washington, DC 20006
Fax: 310-204-0891	202-785-6792

The American Bar Association Commission on Legal Problems of the Elderly and Private Bar Involvement Project

This group will help direct you to attorneys that do pro-bono work for the elderly in your area.

1800 M Street NW
Washington, DC 20036
202-331-2297

National Organization of Social Security Claimants' Representatives

This a membership organization working on behalf of Social Security claimants and beneficiaries. It also holds an annual conference.

6 Prospect Street
Midland Park, NJ 07432
201-444-1415
Fax: 201-444-1823

National Senior Citizens Law Center

This is a support center providing assistance and information to advocates on legal problems for the aged. The center monitors administrative and legislative activities, proposals and keeps attorneys informed of new developments in such areas as age discrimination, government benefits, private pensions, nursing homes and private pensions.

1815 H Street NW, Suite 700	1052 West Sixth Street (7th Fl.)
Washington, DC 20006	Los Angeles, CA 90017
202-887-5280	213-482-3550
Fax: 202-785-6972	Fax: 213-482-8009

Area Agencies for the Aging

Administered by the Administration on Aging, headed by the Assistant Secretary for Aging in the Department of Health and Human Services, these organizations are excellent resources to help you find local senior centers, hospice care providers and legal help. Their job training and community service job programs are especially helpful. Look in your phone book for your local Area for the Aging (see appendix for the main location for your state).

State Insurance Commissioner

Many states have special programs for seniors. For example, some states have enacted partnerships for long-term care which let you protect your money from having to use it all before you can get benefits. Many states have senior divisions for help and fraud prevention. For information on these programs, contact your state insurance commissioner.

American Association of Homes for the Aging

This is a good source of information about living arrangements, homes and projects concerning the elderly.

901 E. Street, NW
Suite 500
Washington, DC 20004-2037
202-783-2242

American Society on Aging

This group is involved in many elder care issues. It is an excellent resource on almost any subject of concern to seniors.

833 Market Street, Suite 512
San Francisco, CA 94103
415-882-2910

Local Senior Centers

Local senior centers that offer workshops, social services and support groups can be invaluable. You can usually find lists of such centers in your phone book.

Veterans Administration

To obtain information on veterans' benefits, and survivor benefits, call 800-827-1000.

National Committee to Preserve Social Security and Medicare

This watchdog organization is fighting hard to maintain Social Security. While you may not agree with all its positions, the group does provide useful information on Social Security. And, you can certainly register your opinions with this group.

2000 K Street NW, Suite 800
Washington, DC 20006
202-822-9459

Tips for avoiding Social Security and Medicare scams and fraud

Unfortunately Social Security and Medicare are not exempt from scams and fraud. Some unscrupulous people specifically try to make money off these programs. The following is some cautionary advice so that you don't get ripped off:

Don't freely give out your Social Security number

You'd be amazed at how easily people give out their Social Security number by putting it on checks, giving it to sales people on the phone, etc. Unless you are dealing with an absolutely reputable organization, *don't give out your Social Security number*. Once you give your number to someone, that person can pretend to be you and apply for credit, use your credit cards, etc. Often, you wouldn't even know this happened unless you checked your credit report. That's why you should check your credit report at least once a year. The three leading credit agencies will provide you with a free credit report if you've been denied credit and TRW will provide you with one free report annually, whether or not you've applied for credit.

The one exception to this rule is that you should make sure you *do* put your Social Security number on all pages of all government documents, such as your tax returns, Social Security forms, etc. You should also make sure you put your name at the top or every page. Often, pages get mixed up when your file is being reviewed.

Be skeptical about paying for Social Security and Medicare help and advice

You shouldn't have to pay government programs for guidance. There are many organizations offering free legal help, counselors, etc. First call the local Social Security number and Medicare hotline. Then call the local Area for the Aging or a local senior center.

Question special doctors' programs that include packages of benefits for Medicare

There have been reports of scams with doctors charging more than the customary Medicare charges. And, still other doctors are asking Medicare patients to sign up for special programs that would cover a wide array of services and medical procedures. The doctors will then charge the patient a "low monthly fee." In most cases, you're already paying the doctors for these services and most of them are covered under Medicare. There's no reason for you to pay double to the doctor. This is another reason why it's so important to know what is covered under Medicare. If you're skeptical about a doctor's plan, check with Medicare before you pay your bill.

Review all official looking bills (especially medical bills) closely

Many types of fraud pertain to being billed for procedures or treatments that you never had. Sometimes, a doctor or nurse will simply circle a treatment from a long list of items, and if more than one item is circled, you're charged again.

Always ask for an itemized list and then review it carefully. You should also review it with an employee at your doctor's office or counselor at the hospital.

If you have a major illness, you will probably get bills from doctors or laboratories that you have never heard of. Don't be intimidated by the number of bills or any threatening letters from bill collection agencies. Keep track of all your bills in your medical log. Get help if you need it to deal with the hospitals and doctors.

You may even get bills that have nothing to do with you. If you're asked to send payment to a P.O. box, check with your doctor or hospital to make sure the bill is legitimate. If you're uncertain, send the person asking for payment a letter saying you have no record of this procedure and you need further explanation.

Finally, sometimes doctors will encourage you to have certain procedures or medical services that aren't medically necessary. The doctors may want to increase their billing. Think about when you have your car fixed: You really don't understand what is must be done to repair your car and the mechanic may bill you for work that isn't necessary. Unfortunately, some doctors do this as well.

You may have heard that many homes are robbed during funerals. It's true. Burglars and scam artists read obituaries. If you have to arrange a funeral, make sure someone stays at the house to avoid break-ins. In addition, you may get anything from fake floral bills, to fake medical bills that look quite official. Again contact counselors or call the Medicare hotline. Don't pay anything until you're sure that you owe the money.

Be careful of institutions that ask you for your Medicare number for supposedly free services

Sometimes, you will hear of an offer from a medical institution offering free services. Chances are, if they asked for your Medicare number, they are billing it to Medicare. This is fraud and costs Medicare a great deal of money and, in turn, leads to higher taxes, higher Medicare co-payments and limited services. If a service is free, there's no reason for you to have to provide your Medicare number.

Watch out for unfair sales practices

Many times, private insurance such as Medicare supplements and disability insurance are necessary. Whatever the type of insurance, you should buy it based on its merits, not because of promises made by an agent. Before buying a policy:

1. Get specimen policies. Read through all the clauses of the policy. If you buy a policy that reads "You are guaranteed that the premium will not rise because of age," you should also check if the premium can increase if you get ill.
2. Get the agent's name, phone number and insurance number. Tell him or her that you make it a standard practice to call the Insurance Commissioner to check credentials, past complaints, etc. You can also check references by asking the agent for names of other clients.
3. Ask for the ratings of the insurance company as well as its phone number. Call the insurance company and check whether you have been given accurate information by the agent.

Don't assume that you have to pay for help reviewing a Medicare claim or getting a job referral. Generally, seniors are able to get free advice and help for almost any legal or financial matter.

Many services are available free for seniors. Don't pay what your tax dollars already entitle you to.

What resources are available should you become the victim of a scam?

Always start with your local Social Security office. You can also contact your local Medicare insurance carrier (see appendix for insurance carrier) or local Peer Review Organization (PRO) (see Appendix C for directory).

If you were denied a claim for Medicare or feel you were treated unfairly by a doctor, their office or medical facility, alert the Medicare Carrier, the Peer Organization and the Health Care Finance Administration.

If you receive fraudulent advertisements or suspicious looking mail, contact your local post office as well as the Chief Postal Inspector:

U.S. Post Office
475 L'Enfant Plaza SW
Washington, DC 20260-2100
202-268-2000

Department of Health and Human Services (Office of Inspector General)

This organization can help you if you feel you've been deceived with regard to your medical treatment or Medicare benefits. The phone number is 800-638-5779.

Elected officials

You voted for your representatives, so you should insist that they listen to your wishes and concerns. Contact your elected officials. Gather friends to join your quest and sign letters collectively. You would be surprised at how much weight a letter with 15 or 20 signatures carries.

State Attorney General

The Attorney General's office can also combat problems regarding fraud and injustices. Contact your Attorney General by writing.

Federal Trade Commission

If you get a call asking you to send money or provide your credit card number, you should be very skeptical. If you think the call is fraudulent, don't fall for it. Contact the Federal Trade Commission Telemarketing Fraud Division.

Telemarketing Fraud
Room 200
6200 Pennsylvania Avenue, NW
Washington, DC 20580

Summary

Remember that you're not alone dealing with Medicare and other government benefits. There are terrific resources available for many different programs. Many help agencies provide invaluable information for free.

In addition, people are robbed of billions of dollars every year. Pay extra attention to make sure that you're not being scammed. Use your common sense and do your homework. If you do end up being scammed, make sure you complain and get help from agencies that can protect you. After all, you have worked too hard for your money to have it taken away by scam artists.

Chapter 15

Other sections of the entitlement programs you should know about

Although the primary focus of the book is on Social Security and Medicare, you should be aware of the other programs available to help you. You may need assistance paying your bills or getting food for your family. There is help available and you should learn how you can get this assistance. Among these programs:

Aid to Families with Dependent Children (AFDC)

This is one of the entitlements enacted as part of the Social Security Act. It is designed to insure that children receive certain benefits that they have been deprived of for various reasons.

To be eligible for benefits, a child must be deprived of parental support or care *and* in need of financial assistance.

To be denied of parental support for purposes of AFDC, the child's parent or parents must have either died, be continually absent from the home, be mentally or physically incapacitated or the principal wage earner must be unemployed.

Financial eligibility

There are specific income and asset tests for requirements that must be met to receive benefits. The amounts vary on where you live, your need and a variety of factors; usually the income limits are quite low.

There are many other requirements that may require a recipient to take part in specific work programs.

If you want to find out if you're eligible for any of these programs in your state, contact either the *Department of Human Resources (Public Assistance Division),* sometimes called *The Department of Health and Social Services for Family Support.*

Food stamps

This program was designed to help low-income people who might otherwise suffer from malnutrition. Unfortunately, there are still millions of elderly people at nutritional risk. There's a high percentage of elderly citizens who could use the Food Stamp program but do not. It may be that the elderly don't want to admit they need help or they are simply unaware of the programs.

If you are eligible for a small benefit, take advantage of it, whether it's for a Meals on Wheels or Nutrition Site program. If you are disabled, scared to go out shopping alone because of crime in your neighborhood or have a very low income, inquire about these benefits by contacting a local Food Stamp Office.

The food stamp program is quite complicated because many states have their own rules. As with all the programs discussed in this book, you should find a local resource that understands the particulars in your community.

In most cases the amount you can earn and still qualify for food stamp benefits is fairly low, but the numbers differ depending on the number of dependents in your household, the year and other factors.

Meals on Wheels and Nutrition Site meals

This benefit provides meals for free or at reduced rates. Any person over 60 can apply for this benefit. Many states and communities do not have an income restriction.

If your community has a Meals on Wheels program, you may be eligible for one free meal per day, either delivered or at a specific site. Often, the requirements for this service are not stringent.

Contact the local *Department of Human Services* (or equivalent department) to find out whether your community has a program and what are the eligibility rules. Some of these programs are operated in conjunction with the local Area for the Aging.

Low-Income Home Energy Assistance Program (LIHEAP)

This program will usually pay a one-time payment to cover your heating expenses. To find out if there's program in your area and whether you qualify, contact the local Department of Public Works.

Call and ride programs, senior citizens' rail discounts, etc.

Free or low cost transportation services are available in many communities. Sometimes, you have to be age 60; in other locations, age 65, in order to qualify. If you have a disability, you may qualify at a lower age. Contact your local Area for the Aging and inquire about these benefits. Ask your local bus or railroad company whether they have any special senior programs.

Summary

Statistics about the problems of the elderly are alarming, from the number of seniors who die of malnutrition to the people who can't afford to heat their apartments in winter. However, in most cases, there are services or agencies that can help seniors avoid these problems. Although it can be difficult to find out which services are available in your community and whether you qualify, it is well worth the effort.

Chapter 16

Future of Social Security and Medicare

This country faces a major problem that can no longer be ignored or denied. Entitlement programs are among the biggest part of the federal budget. Actually, Medicare and Social Security have separate trust funds that can only be used to provide assistance for workers and their families who qualify for these programs. Experts say there is enough money in the Social Security Trust to pay out benefits for another 40 years, while the Medicare trust funds have just a few years left before the money runs out. The Social Security trust fund has about 350 million dollars, which is the highest amount in nearly 20 years.

Medicaid and Social Security funds come out of the general treasury budget. Congress appropriates the funds for these programs, while the Social Security Administration administers the programs.

Now that the Social Security Administration is independent, it should have more autonomy in its administration. Hopefully, Social Security and Medicare will not be lumped in with other programs that Congress is trying to cut back. Still, there are concerns that there will have to be a dramatic overhaul in the Social Security system. Some people are calling for a much needed increase in benefits. However, the taxes that would have to be imposed on the population could be a major burden. Let's examine in depth the proposals to change these systems.

Social Security and Medicare

For all practical purposes Social Security and Medicare are self-supporting, which means they're not adding to our deficit. In fact, the trust fund that Social

Security and Medicare taxes go into actually operates at a surplus, although the Social Security trust fund is better funded than Medicare's. Most experts don't expect the surplus to disappear until about the year 2030. By then, with higher taxes, more workers and lower benefits, the surplus would again be built up.

However, the benefits for the programs appear to be only marginal. The possible Social Security reforms don't seem to offer much to seniors.

My thoughts on what an overhauled Social Security system would be:

I feel that Social Security is a poor investment. First of all, you have to pay a tax that is not capped. The more you make, the more you pay. But, your benefits don't reflect this higher contribution—they are capped. Assume that a single high-income worker born in 1957 who lives to age 80 will probably pay more than *half* of all the benefits he or she will receive. This results in a negative return on the money. The same rate in most money market accounts would be a better return. Assume you entered the work force and earned an annual salary in the low $20,000 range and received normal raises. By the time you retired, you would receive roughly $12,500 per year (in today's dollars) in Social Security benefits. However, if you took your FICA tax and simply invested it yourself to make, say 6 percent (government bonds are paying higher than this), you would have a savings of over $800,000. If you had $800,000, you could probably take four or five times what you would have received per year in Social Security and had extra principal.

If you took the same money you paid into Social Security and invested it wisely, contributed to a company retirement plan or simply bought United States zero-coupon bonds coming due in the years you planned on retiring, you would receive five times as much money as you would receive from Social Security.

Not only are you and I taxed under Social Security, but if you make too much money *during* retirement you're taxed again. Further, it reduces the benefits, which again brings up the question whether or not Social Security is a good investment. Most of you simply can't afford to "retire" full time, so you work. If you work, your Social Security retirement benefits may be reduced. It's a vicious cycle.

I think that Social Security should be optional. You should be able to choose to opt out of Social Security and Medicare. I believe there should be some type of extended pension plan in which you could take the funds that would have gone into FICA (Social Security Contributions) and contribute to a special private pension and either get a tax-benefit for the contribution, or retire and get back tax-free benefits. By doing this, you would waive rights to all services under Social Security. The system could be set up so that you could still have Medicare or a similar health plan (through the funds saved in this special pension plan). You would still have to contribute a special tax into Social Security to help pay for those entitlement programs that actually increase our Federal budget. Paying one to three percent toward Social Security that I opted out of would not be a problem, because, by opting out and saving the money on your own, you'll get more benefits than in our current system.

If this never happens (and it isn't likely), I think that the money in the Social Security trust fund should be invested more astutely. The only investment this trust fund makes is in special Government bonds. However, with some simple financial planning, the billions of dollars that are currently in the Social Security Trust fund could earn millions more in interest. Think of all the ways the trust funds could earn more money: they could purchase longer-term government bonds, zero-coupons, invest in Ginnie Maes and even stocks and bonds.

In terms of Medicare, more money should be put into education and preventative programs which would probably reduce costly medical procedures because the procedures wouldn't be needed as often.

The probable future of Social Security

I don't think my proposals will be enacted. What is more likely to happen is a combination of different plans.

The government will be forced to learn how to keep costs under control. Taxes for Social Security and Medicare will continue to rise. The benefits will start later and later and will increase much more slowly, slower than the pace of inflation. You will also see a reduction in benefits ranging from more stringent disability rules, to tougher qualifying limitations for Medicaid.

In fact, Rep. Dan Rostenkowski (D-Ill.) has introduced a bill that would again raise taxes and reduce benefits to ensure the system is solvent for at least another 75 years. This is unfortunate since the system is already at the point that it barely pays a benefit now.

I think most of us agree that reform is necessary. The question is just how should this be done?

The future of Medicare

I have no doubt that the Medicare system will change dramatically over the next five years.

Medicare is losing money and costing the taxpayers and the government a great deal of money. Think of the system as a mushroom. We have a retiring population that is living longer and spending more money on Medicare. Conversely, we have a smaller workforce and therefore, not as many people are paying into Medicare. So, what is going to happen?

Medicare will be broke by the year 2002 if it continues as it exists today. Congress has said that it plans to cut future Medicare spending. That may be fine in theory but where do you cut? It seems to me that our lawmakers will be pushing us more and more to use managed care for Medicare. Currently, the most popular form of managed care is the Health Maintenance Organization (HMO). This seems like a viable alternative, but the amount that Medicare will pay to the HMOs will be cut. Therefore, in order to be profitable, the HMOs will probably limit the services and procedures they allow.

In addition, it's likely that individuals will be responsible for larger co-payments, higher premiums and higher deductibles. Medicare and the HMOs will then cover fewer and fewer Medicare services. Services such as limited home-health care and skilled nursing care could be on the brink of extinction.

Since, unfortunately, these costs seem inevitable, we need to be ready. Since more of our own money will have to go toward paying for health care, we should budget and save so that we have money for health care expenses. And, we should all learn about HMOs since we will be using them more in the future.

The bottom line is that Medicare will change. It's not certain how it will change but rest assured that the changes will not be in our favor. Be prepared!

Summary

Social Security, Medicare and other entitlement programs are wonderful benefits but they are beginning to cost so much and with benefits continuing to be reduced, the value of the system is diminishing. To continue these programs, we need to take a proactive role, develop a plan and implement it.

When our lawmakers talk about raising our Social Security Tax (FICA) or cutting benefits again, don't stand for it. Speak up and say what's on your mind. You are probably a better manager of your money than the government. Fight it, don't let them continue to rip you off!

Appendix A

Agencies on the aging and insurance counseling

Each state has its own laws and regulations governing all types of insurance. The agencies on aging are responsible for coordinating services for older Americans. The telephone number(s) are to call for insurance counseling services. Calls to the following 800 numbers are free when made within their respective states.

Alabama

Commission on Aging
770 Washington Ave., Suite 470
P.O. Box 301851
Montgomery, AL 36130
1-800-243-5463, 205-242-5743

Alaska

Older Alaskans Commission
P.O. Box 110209
Juneau, AK 99811-0209
1-800-478-6065
907-562-7249, 907-465-3250

Arizona

Dept. of Economic Security
Aging & Adult Administration
1789 W. Jefferson St.
Phoenix, AZ 85007
1-800-432-4040, 602-542-4446

Arkansas

Div. of Aging and Adult Services
1417 Donaghey Plaza South
P.O. Box 1437/Slot 1412
Little Rock, AR 72203-1437
1-800-852-5494
501-686-2940, 501-682-2441

California

Department of Aging
1600 K St.
Sacramento, CA 95814
1-800-927-4357
916-323-7315, 916-322-3887

Colorado

Aging and Adult Services
Department of Social Services
1575 Sherman St., 4th Fl.
Denver, CO 80203-1714
303-894-7499, ext. 356
303-866-3851

Connecticut

Elderly Services Division
175 Main St.
Hartford, CT 06106
1-800 443-9946, 203-566-7772

Delaware

Division of Aging
Dept. of Health & Social Services
1901 N. DuPont Hwy.
2nd Floor Annex Admin.
New Castle, DE 19720
1-800-336-9500, 302-577-4791

District of Columbia

Office on Aging
441 4th St. NW, 9th Fl.
Washington, DC 20001
202-994-7463
202-724-5626, 202-724-5622

Florida

Department of Elder Affairs
1317 Winewood Boulevard
Building 1, Room 317
Tallahassee, FL 32399-0700
904-922-2073, 904-922-5297

Georgia

Division of Aging Services
Dept. of Human Resources
2 Peachtree St. NW, Rm. 18.403
Atlanta, GA 30303
1-800-669-8387, 404-657-5258

Hawaii

Executive Office on Aging
335 Merchant St., Room 241
Honolulu, HI 96813
808-586-0100

Idaho

Office on Aging
Statehouse, Room 108
Boise, ID 83720
1-800-247-4422

Illinois

Department on Aging
421 E. Capitol Ave.
Springfield, IL 62701
1-800-252-8966, 217-785-3356

Indiana

Div. of Aging & Home Services
402 W. Washington St.
P.O. Box 7083
Indianapolis, IN 46207-7083
1-800-545-7763, 1-800-452-4800
317-232-7020

Iowa

Department of Elder Affairs
Jewett Building, Suite 236
914 Grand Ave.
Des Moines, IA 50309
515-281-5705, 515-281-5187

Kansas

Department on Aging
150-S. Docking State Office Bldg.
915 S.W. Harrison
Topeka, KS 66612-1500
1-800-432-3535, 913-296-4986

Kentucky

Division of Aging Services
Cabinet for Human Resources
275 E. Main St., 5th Fl. West
Frankfort, KY 40621
1-800-372-2991, 502-564-6930

Louisiana

Governor's Off. of Elderly Affairs
4550 N. Boulevard
P.O. Box 80374
Baton Rouge, LA 70896-0374
1-800-259-5301
504-342-5301, 504-925-1700

Maine

Bureau of Elder and Adult Services
State House, Station 11
Augusta, ME 04333
1-800-750-5353, 207-624-5335

Maryland

Office on Aging
301 W. Preston St., Room 1004
Baltimore, MD 21201
1-800-243-3425, 410-225-1102

Massachusetts

Executive Office of Elder Affairs
1 Ashburton Place, 5th Fl.
Boston, MA 02108
1-800-882-2003, 617-727-7750

Michigan

Office of Services to the Aging
611 W. Ottawa St.
P.O. Box 30026
Lansing, MI 48909
517-373-8230

Minnesota

Board on Aging
Human Services Bldg., 4th Fl.
444 Lafayette Road
St. Paul, MN 55155-3843
1-800-882-6262, 612-296-2770

Mississippi

Div. of Aging & Adult Services
750 N. State St.
Jackson, MS 39202
1-800-948-3090, 601-359-4929

Missouri

Div. of Aging—Dept. of Social Svces.
P.O. Box 1337
615 Howerton Court
Jefferson City, MO 65102-1337
1-800-390-3330, 314-751-3082

Montana

Office on Aging
48 N. Last Chance Gulch
P.O. Box 8005
Helena, MT 59620
1-800-332-2272, 406-444-5900

Nebraska

Department of Aging
State Office Building
301 Centennial Mall S.
Lincoln, NE 68509-5044
402-471-4506, 402-471-2306

Nevada

Dept. of Human Resources
Division of Aging Services
340 N. 11th St., Suite 114
Las Vegas, NV 89101
1-800-307-4444
702-367-1218, 702-486-3545

New Hampshire

Dept. of Health & Human Services
Div. of Elderly & Adult Services
State Office Park S.
115 Pleasant St.
Annex Building No. 1
Concord, NH 03301
603-271-4642, 603-271-4680

New Jersey

Dept. of Community Affairs
Division on Aging
S. Broad and Front streets
CN 807
Trenton, NJ 08625-0807
1-800-792-8820, 609-984-3951

New Mexico

State Agency on Aging
La Villa Rivera Building
224 E. Palace Ave.
Santa Fe, NM 87501
1-800-432-2080, 505-827-7640

New York

State Office for the Aging
2 Empire State Plaza
Albany, NY 12223-0001
1-800-333-4114, 1-800-342-9871
518-474-5731

North Carolina

Division of Aging
693 Palmer Dr.
Caller Box 29531
Raleigh, NC 27626-0531
1-800-443-9354, 919-733-3983

North Dakota

Department of Human Services
Aging Services Division
P.O. Box 7070
Bismarck, ND 58507-7070
1-800-247-0560, 701-224-2577

Ohio

Department of Aging
50 W. Broad St., 9th Fl.
Columbus, OH 43266-0501
1-800-686-1578, 1-800-282-1206
615-466-1221

Oklahoma

Department of Human Services
Aging Services Division
312 N.E. 28th St.
Oklahoma City, OK 73125
405-521-2327, 405-521-6628

Oregon

Dept. of Human Resources
Senior & Disabled Services Div.
500 Summer St., NE, 2nd Fl.
Salem, OR 97310-1015
1-800-722-4134, 503-378-4728

Pennsylvania

Department of Aging
400 Market St.
State Office Building
Harrisburg, PA 17101
717-783-8975, 717-783-1550

Rhode Island

Department of Elderly Affairs
160 Pine St.
Providence, RI 02903
1-800-322-2880, 401-277-2858

South Carolina

Division on Aging
202 Arbor Lake Dr., Suite 301
Columbia, SC 29223-4554
1-800-868-9095, 803-737-7500

South Dakota

Office of Adult Services & Aging
700 Governors Dr.
Pierre, SD 57501-2291
605-773-3656

Tennessee

Commission on Aging
706 Church St., Suite 201
Nashville, TN 37243-0860
1-800-525-2816, 615-741-2056

Texas

Department on Aging
P.O. Box 12786 (787711)
1949 IH 35 S.
Austin, TX 78741
1-800-252-3439, 1-800-252-9240
512-444-2727

Utah

Division of Aging and Adult
Services
120 North 200 West
P.O. Box 45500
Salt Lake City, UT 84145-0500
801-538-3910

Vermont

Dept. of Aging & Disabilities
Waterbury Complex
103 S. Main St.
Waterbury, VT 05671-2301
1-800-642-5119, 802-241-2400

Virginia

Department for the Aging
700 Centre, 10th Fl.
700 E. Franklin St.
Richmond, VA 23219-2327
1-800-552-4464, 804-225-2271

Washington

Aging & Adult Services Admin.
Department of Social & Health
Services
P.O. Box 45050
Olympia, WA 98504-5050
1-800-397-4422, 206-586-3768

West Virginia

Commission on Aging
State Capitol Complex
Holly Grove
1900 Kanawha Blvd. E.
Charleston, WV 25305-0160
304-558-3317

Wisconsin

Board on Aging and
Long-Term Care
214 N. Hamilton St.
Madison, WI 53703
1-800-242-1060, 608-266-8944

Wyoming

Division on Aging
Hathaway Building
2300 Capitol Ave., Room 139
Cheyenne, WY 82002
1-800-442-2766, 1-800-438-5768
307-777-7986

American Samoa

Territorial Admin. on Aging
Government of American Samoa
Pago Pago, AS 96799
684-633-1252

Commonwealth of the Northern Mariana Islands

Department of Community and
Cultural Affairs Civic Center
Commonwealth of the Northern
Mariana Islands
Saipan, CM 96950
607-234-6011

Federated States of Micronesia

State Agency on Aging
Office of Health Services
Federated States of Micronesia
Ponape, E.C.I. 96941

Guam

Division of Senior Citizens
Department of Public Health and
Social Services
P.O. Box 2816
Agana, Guam 96910
011 (671) 734-4361

Palau

State Agency on Aging
Department of Social Services
Republic of Palau
Koror, Palau 96940

Puerto Rico

Governor's Office of Elderly Affairs
Gericulture Commission
Box 11398
Santurce, PR 00910
809-721-5710, 809-722-2429

Republic of the Marshall Islands

State Agency on Aging
Department of Social Services
Republic of the Marshall Islands
Marjuro, Marshall Islands 96960

Virgin Islands

Senior Citizen Affairs Division
Department of Human Services
19 Estate Diamond, Fredericksted
St. Croix, VI 00840
809-774-2991, 809-772-0930

Appendix B

Medicare carriers

Carriers can answer questions about medical insurance (Part B)

The toll-free or 800 numbers listed below can usually be used only in the states where the carriers are located. Also listed are the local commercial numbers for the carriers. Out-of-state callers may use the commercial numbers.

These carrier toll-free numbers are for beneficiaries and should not be used by doctors and suppliers.

Many carriers have installed automated telephone answering systems. If you have a touch-tone telephone, you can follow the system instructions to find out about your latest claims and get other information. If you do not have a touch-tone telephone, stay on the line and someone will help you.

Alabama

Medicare/Blue Cross-Blue Shield of Alabama
P.O. Box 830140
Birmingham, AL 35283-0140
1-800-292-8855
205-988-2244

Alaska

Medicare/Aetna Life Ins. Co.
200 S.W. Market St.
P.O. Box 1998
Portland, OR 97207-1998
Toll-free Alaska to Oregon customer service site: 1-800-452-0125
Customer service in Oregon: 503-222-6831

Arizona

Medicare/Aetna Life Ins. Co.
P.O. Box 37200
Phoenix, AZ 85069
1-800-352-0411 *cannot be reached from San Diego*
602-861-1968

Arkansas

Medicare/Arkansas Blue Cross & Blue Shield
P.O. Box 1418
Little Rock, AR 72203-1418
1-800-482-5525 *cannot be reached from San Diego*
501-378-2320

California

Counties of Los Angeles, Orange, San Diego, Ventura, Imperial, San Luis Obispo, Santa Barbara:
Medicare/Transamerica Occidental Life Insurance Co.
Box 30540
Los Angeles, CA 90030-0540
1-800-675-2266, 213-748-2311
Rest of state:
Medicare Claims Dept.
Blue Shield of California
Chico, CA 95976
In area codes 209, 408, 415, 510, 707, 916:
1-800-952-8627, 916-743-1587
In the following area codes—other than Los Angeles, Orange, San Diego, Ventura, Imperial, San Luis Obispo and Santa Barbara counties: 213, 310, 619, 714, 805, 818, 909:
1-800-848-7713, 714-796-9393

Colorado

Medicare/Blue Cross & Blue Shield of Colorado
Coordination of Benefits:
P.O. Box 173550
Denver, CO 80217
Correspondence/appeals:
P.O. Box 173500
Denver, CO 80217
Metro Denver 303-894-5600
In Colorado, outside of metro area: 1-800-332-6681

Connecticut

Medicare/The Travelers Companies
538 Preston Avenue
P.O. Box 9000
Meriden, CT 06454-9000
1-800-982-6819
In Hartford: 203-728-6783
In Meriden area: 203-237-8592

Delaware

Medicare/Pennsylvania Blue Shield
P.O. Box 890200
Camp Hill, PA 17089-0200
1-800-851-3535

District of Columbia

Medicare/Pennsylvania Blue Shield
P.O. Box 890100
Camp Hill, PA 17089-0100
1-800-233-1124

Florida

Medicare/Blue Cross & Blue Shield of Florida, Inc.
P.O. Box 2360
Jacksonville, FL 32231

Copies of Explanation of Your Medicare Part B Benefits notices, requests for MEDPAR directories, claims inquiries (status or verification of receipt) and address changes:
904-355-8899

Georgia

Medicare/Aetna Life Ins. Co.
P.O. Box 3018
Savannah, GA 31402-3018
1-800-727-0827, 912-920-2412

Hawaii

Medicare/Aetna Life Ins. Co.
P.O. Box 3947
Honolulu, HI 96812
808-524-1240

Idaho

Connecticut General Life Ins. Co.
3150 N. Lakeharbor Lane
Suite 254
P.O. Box 8048
Boise, ID 83707-6219
208-342-7763

Illinois

Medicare Claims/Health Care Services Corporation
P.O. Box 4422
Marion, IL 62959
312-938-8000

Indiana

Medicare Part B/AdminaStar Federal
P.O. Box 7073
Indianapolis, IN 46207
1-800-622-4792, 317-842-4151

Iowa

Medicare/IASD Health Services Corporation
(d/b/a Blue Cross & Blue Shield of Iowa)
636 Grand
Des Moines, IA 50309
1-800-532-1285, 515-245-4785

Kansas

Counties of Johnson and Wyandotte:
Medicare/Blue Cross & Blue Shield of Kansas, Inc.
P.O. Box 419840
Kansas City, MO 64141-6840
1-800-892-5900, 816-561-0900
Rest of state:
Medicare/Blue Cross & Blue of Kansas, Inc.
1133 S.W. Topeka Blvd.
P.O. Box 239
Topeka, KS 66629-0001
913-232-3773

Kentucky

Medicare—Part B/Blue Cross & Blue Shield of Kentucky, Inc.
100 E. Vine St.
Lexington, KY 40507
1-800-999-7608, 502-425-6759

Louisiana

Arkansas Blue Cross & Blue Shield, Inc.

Medicare Administration
P.O. Box 83830
Baton Rouge, LA 70884-3830
In New Orleans: 504-529-1494
In Baton Rouge: 504-927-3490

Maine

Medicare/C and S Administrative Services
P.O. Box 1000
Hingham, MA 02044-9191
For non-assigned claims:
P.O. Box 2222
Hingham, MA 02044-9193
1-800-492-0919, 207-828-4300

Maryland

Counties of Montgomery, Prince Georges:
Medicare/Pennsylvania Blue Shield
P.O. Box 890100
Camp Hill, PA 17089-0100
1-800-233-1124
Rest of state:
Blue Cross & Blue Shield of Maryland, Inc.
1946 Greenspring Dr.
Timonium, MD 21093
1-800-492-4795
Providers: 410-771-6111
All others: 410-581-3000

Massachusetts

Medicare/C and S Administrative Services
P.O. Box 1000
Hingham, MA 02044-9191
For non-assigned claims:
P.O. Box 2222
Hingham, MA 02044-9193
1-800-882-1228, 617-741-3300

Michigan

Medicare Part B
Blue Cross & Blue Shield of Michigan
P.O. Box 2201
Detroit, MI 48231-2201
1-800-482-4045, 313-225-8200

Minnesota

Counties of Anoka, Dakota, Fillmore, Goodhue, Hennepin, Houston, Olmstead, Ramsey, Wabasha, Washington, Winona:
Medicare/The Travelers Ins. Co.
8120 Penn Avenue S.
Bloomington, MN 55431
612-884-7171
Rest of state:
Medicare/Blue Cross & Blue Shield of Minnesota
P.O. Box 64357
St. Paul, MN 55164
1-800-392-0343, 612-456-5070

Mississippi

Medicare/The Travelers Ins. Co.
P.O. Box 22545
Jackson, MS 39225-2545
601-956-0372

Missouri

Counties of Andrew, Atchison, Bates, Benton, Buchanan, Caldwell, Carroll, Cass, Clay, Clinton, Daviess, DeKalb, Gentry, Grundy, Harrison, Henry, Holt, Jackson, Johnson, Lafayette, Livingston, Mercer, Nodaway, Pettis, Plat, Ray, St. Clair, Saline, Vernon, Worth:

Medicare/Blue Cross & Blue
Shield of Kansas, Inc.
> P.O. Box 419840
> Kansas City, MO 64141-6840
> *Rest of state:*
> Medicare
> General American Life Ins. Co.
> P.O. Box 505
> St. Louis, MO 63166
> 314-843-8880

Montana

Medicare/Blue Cross & Blue
Shield of Montana, Inc.
> 2501 Beltview
> P.O. Box 4310
> Helena, MT 59605
> 406-444-8350

Nebraska

The carrier is Blue Cross and Blue Shield of Kansas, Inc. Claims, however, should be sent to:
> Medicare Part B
> Blue Cross/Blue Shield
of Nebraska
> P.O. Box 3106
> Omaha, NE 68103-0106
> *Customer service site in Kansas:*
913-232-3773

Nevada

Medicare/Aetna Life Ins. Co.
> P.O. Box 37230
> Phoenix, AZ 85069
> 602-861-1968

New Hampshire

Medicare/C and S Administrative Services
> P.O. Box 1000
> Hingham, MA 02044-9191
> *For non-assigned claims:*
> P.O. Box 2222
> Hingham, MA 02044-9193
> 1-800-447-1142, 207-828-4300

New Jersey

Medicare/Pennsylvania
Blue Shield
> P.O. Box 400010
> Harrisburg, PA 17140-0010
> 1-800-462-9306, 717-975-7333

New Mexico

Medicare/Aetna Life Ins. Co.
> P.O. Box 25500
> Oklahoma City, OK 73125-0500
> 1-800-423-2925
> *In Albuquerque:* 505-821-3350,
505-843-9379

New York

Counties of Bronx, Columbia, Delaware, Dutchess, Greene, Kings, Nassau, New York, Orange, Putnam, Richmond, Rockland, Suffolk, Sullivan, Ulster, Westchester:
> Medicare B/Empire Blue Cross
& Blue Shield

P.O. Box 2280
Peekskill, NY 10566
1-800-442-8430, 516-244-5100
County of Queens:
Medicare/Group Health, Inc.
P.O. Box 1608, Ansonia Station
New York, NY 10023
212-721-1770
Rest of state:
Blue Shield of Western New York
Upstate Medicare Div.-Part B
7-9 Court St.
Binghamton, NY 13901-3197

North Carolina

Connecticut General Life Ins. Co.
P.O. Box 671
Nashville, TN 37202
1-800-672-3071, 919-665-0348

North Dakota

Medicare/Blue Shield of North
Dakota
4510 13th Ave., S.W.
Fargo, ND 58121-0001
1-800-247-2267, 701-282-0691

Ohio

Medicare/Nationwide Mutual
Insurance Co.
P.O. Box 57
Columbus, OH 43216
614-249-7157

Oklahoma

Medicare/Aetna Life Ins. Co.
701 N.W. 63rd St.
Oklahoma City, OK 73116-7693
1-800-522-9079, 405-848-7711

Oregon

Medicare/Aetna Life Ins. Co.
200 S.W. Market Street
P.O. Box 1997
Portland, OR 87207-1997
1-800-452-0125, 503-222-6831

Pennsylvania

Medicare/Pennsylvania
Blue Shield
P.O. Box 890065
Camp Hill, PA 17089-0065
1-800-382-1274, 717-763-3601

Rhode Island

Medicare/Blue Cross & Blue
Shield of Rhode Island
Inquiry Department
444 Westminster St.
Providence, RI 02903-3279
1-800-662-5170, 401-861-2273

South Carolina

Medicare Part B
Blue Cross & Blue Shield of
South Carolina
P.O. Box 100190
Columbia, SC 29202
1-800-868-2522, 803-788-3882

South Dakota

Medicare Part B/Blue Shield of
North Dakota
4510 13th Avenue, S.W.
Fargo, ND 58121-0001
1-800-437-4762, 701-282-0691

Tennessee

Connecticut General Life Ins. Co.
P.O. Box 1465
Nashville, TN 372020
615-244-5650

Texas

Medicare/Blue Cross & Blue
Shield of Texas, Inc.
P.O. Box 660031
Dallas, TX 75266-0031
1-800-442-2620

Utah

Medicare/Blue Shield of Utah
P.O. Box 30269
Salt Lake City, UT 84130-0269
801-481-6196

Vermont

Medicare/C and S Adminis-
trative Services
P.O. Box 1000
Hingham, MA 02044-9191
For non-assigned claims:
P.O. Box 2222
Hingham, MA 02044-9193
1-800-447-1142, 207-828-4300

Virginia

Counties of Arlington, Fairfax:
Cities of Alexandria, Falls
Church, Fairfax:
Medicare/Pennsylvania
Blue Shield
P.O. Box 890100
Camp Hill, PA 17089-0100
1-800-233-1124
717-763-3601

Rest of state:
Medicare/The Travelers Ins. Co.
P.O. Box 26463
Richmond, VA 23261
804-330-4786

Washington

Aetna Life Insurance Company
Medicare Part B
P.O. Box 91099
Seattle, WA 89111-9199
1-800-372-6604
In Seattle: 206-621-0359

West Virginia

Medicare/Nationwide Mutual
Insurance Co.
P.O. Box 57
Columbus, OH 43216
614-249-7157

Wisconsin

Medicare/WPS
Box 1787
Madison, WI 53701
In Madison: 608-221-3330

Wyoming

Blue Cross & Blue Shield of
North Dakota
P.O. Box 628
Cheyenne, WY 82003
1-800-442-2371, 307-632-9381

American Samoa

Medicare/Aetna Life Ins. Co.
P.O. Box 3947
Honolulu, HI 96812
808-524-1240

Northern Mariana Islands

Medicare/Aetna Life Ins. Co.
P.O. Box 3947
Honolulu, HI 96812
808-524-1240

Virgin Islands

Medicare/Seguros De Servicio
De Salud De Puerto Rico
P.O. Box 71391
San Juan, PR 00936-1391

Puerto Rico

Medicare/Seguros De Servicio
De Salud De Puerto Rico
P.O. Box 71391
San Juan, PR 00936-1391
In Puerto Rico: 800-981-7015
In Puerto Rico metro area:
809-749-4900

Appendix C

Medicare Peer Review Organizations (PROs)

PROs can answer questions about the quality of care and access to care in a Medicare-certified facility. PROs cannot answer questions about your bill or about what Medicare covers. For Part A or Part B billing or coverage questions, call your Part B carrier or Part A intermediary. Carriers are listed for your referral.

(*) PRO will accept collect calls from out of state on this number.

Alabama

Alabama Quality Assurance
Foundation, Inc.
Suite 200 N. 1 Perimeter Park S.
Birmingham, AL 35243-2327
1-800-760-3540

Alaska

PRO-West
(PRO for Alaska)
10700 Meridian Ave. N., Ste. 100
Seattle, WA 98133-9075
1-800-445-6941
in Anchorage: 562-2252

Arizona

Health Svces. Advisory Group, Inc.
301 E. Bethany Home Rd., B-157
Phoenix, AZ 85012
1-800-626-1577
in Arizona: 1-800-359-9909 or
1-800-223-6693

Arkansas

Arkansas Foundation for
Medical Care, Inc.
P.O. Box 2424
809 Garrison Ave.
Fort Smith, AR 72902
1-800-824-7586
in Arkansas: 1-800-272-5528

California

California Medical Review, Inc.
60 Spear St., Suite 500
San Francisco, CA 94105
1-800-841-1602 *in-state only*
1-415-882-5800*

Colorado

Colorado Fdn. for Medical Care
Pavilion Towers II
2821 S. Parker Road
P.O. Box 17300
Denver, CO 80217-0300
1-800-727-7086 *in-state only*
1-303-695-3333*

Connecticut

Connecticut PRO, Inc.
100 Roscommon Drive, Ste. 200
Middletown, CT 06457
1-800-553-7590 *in-state only*
1-203-632-2008*

Delaware

West Virginia Medical Inst., Inc.
(PRO for Delaware)
3001 Chesterfield Place
Charleston, WV 25304
1-800-642-8686 ext. 266
in Wilmington: 655-3077

District of Columbia

Delmarva Foundation for Medical Care, Inc.
(PRO for DC)
9240 Centreville Road
Eason, MD 21601
1-800-645-0011
in Maryland: 1-800-492-5811

Florida

Florida Medical Quality
Assurance, Inc.
1211 N. Westshore Blvd., Ste. 700
Tampa, FL 33607
1-800-844-0795 *in-state only*
813-281-9024

Georgia

Georgia Medical Care Foundation
57 Executive Park S., Suite 200
Atlanta, GA 30329
1-800-282-2614 *in-state only*
404-982-0411

Hawaii

Hawaii Medical Service Assn.
(PRO for American Samoa/
Guam and Hawaii)
818 Keeaumoku St.
P.O. Box 860
Honolulu, HI 96808-0860
1-808-944-3586*

Idaho

PRO-West (PRO for Idaho)
10700 Meridian Ave. N., Ste. 100
Seattle, WA 98133-9075
1-800-445-6941
Boise/collect: 1-208-343-4617*

Illinois

Crescent Counties Foundation
for Medical Care
1001 Warrenville Road
Lisle, IL 60532
1-800-647-8089, 708-769-9600

Indiana

Indiana Medical Review
Organization
2901 Ohio Blvd., Box 3713
Terre Haute, IN 47803
1-800-288-1499

Iowa

Iowa Fdn. for Medical Care
6000 Westown Pkwy., Ste. 350E
West Des Moines, IA 50266-7771
1-800-752-7014, 515-223-2900

Kansas

The Kansas Foundation for
Medical Care, Inc.
2947 SW Wanamaker Drive
Topeka, KS 66614
1-800-432-0407 *in-state only*
913-273-2552

Kentucky

Kentucky Medical Review
Organization
10503 Timberwood Cir., Ste. 200
P.O. Box 23540
Louisville, KY 40223
1-800-288-1499

Louisiana

Louisiana Health Care Rev., Inc.
8591 United Plaza Boulevard
Suite 270
Baton Rouge, LA 70809
1-800-433-4958 *in-state only*
504-926-6353

Maine

Health Care Review, Inc.
(PRO for Maine)
Henry C. Hall Building
345 Blackstone Blvd.
Providence, RI 02906
1-800-541-9888, 1-800-528-0700
both numbers in Maine only
1-207-945-0244*

Maryland

Delmarva Foundation for Medical Care, Inc.
(PRO for Maryland)
9240 Centreville Road
Easton, MD 21601
1-800-645-0011
in Maryland: 1-800-492-5811

Massachusetts

Massachusetts PRO, Inc.
235 Wyman St.
Waltham, MA 02154-1231
1-800-252-5533 *in-state only*
1-617-890-0011*

Michigan

Michigan PRO
40600 Ann Arbor Road, Ste. 200
Plymouth, MI 48170-4495
1-800-365-5899

Minnesota

Fdn. for Health Care Evaluation
2901 Metro Drive Suite 400
Bloomington, MN 55425
1-800-444-3423

Mississippi

Mississippi Foundation for
Medical Care, Inc.
P.O. Box 4665
735 Riverside Drive
Jackson, MS 39296-4665
1-800-844-0600 *in-state only*
601-948-8894

Missouri

Missouri Patient Care Rev. Fdn.
505 Hobbs Road, Suite 100
Jefferson City, MO 65109
1-800-347-1016

Montana

Montana-Wyoming Foundation
for Medical Care
400 North Park, 2nd Fl.
Helena, MT 59601
1-800-497-8232 *in-state only*
1-406-443-4020*

Nebraska

The Sunderbruch Corp.-N.E.
1221 "N" Street, Suite 800
Lincoln, NE 68508
1-800-247-3004 *in-state only*
1-402-474-7471*

Nevada

Nevada Peer Review
675 E. 2100 South, Suite 270
Salt Lake City, UT 84106-1864
1-800-558-0829 *in Nevada only*
in Reno: 1-702-826-1996
1-702-385-9933*

New Hampshire

New Hampshire Foundation for
Medical Care
15 Old Rollinsford Road, Ste. 302
Dover, NH 03820
1-800-582-7174 *in-state only*
1-603-749-1641*

New Jersey

The PRO of New Jersey, Inc.
Central Division
Brier Hill Court, Building J
East Brunswick, NJ 08816
1-800-624-4557 *in-state only*
1-201-238-5570*

New Mexico

New Mexico Medical Rev. Assn.
707 Broadway NE, Suite 200
P.O. Box 27449
Albuquerque, NM 87125-7449
1-800-432-6824 *in-state only*
505-842-6236
in Albuquerque: 842-6236

New York

Island Peer Review Org., Inc.
1979 Marcus Avenue, 1st Fl.
Lake Success, NY 11042
1-800-331-7767 *in-state only*
1-516-326-7767*

North Carolina

Medical Rev. of North Carolina
5625 Dillard Drive, Suite 203
P.O. Box 37309
Cary, NC 27511-9227
1-800-682-2650 *in-state only*
919-851-2955

North Dakota

North Dakota Health Care
Review, Inc.
900 North Broadway, Suite 301
Minot, ND 58701
1-800-472-2902 *in-state only*
1-701-852-4231*

Ohio

Peer Review Systems, Inc.
P.O. Box 6174
757 Brooksedge Plaza Drive
Weserville, OH 43081-6174
1-800-837-0664
1-800-589-7337 *in-state only*

Oklahoma

Oklahoma Fdn. for Peer Rev., Inc.
Suite 400, The Paragon Building
5801 Broadway Extension
Oklahoma City, OK 73118-7489
1-800-522-3414 *in-state only*
405-840-2981

Oregon

Oregon Medical PRO
1220 S. Morrison, Suite 200
Portland, OR 97205
1-800-344-4354 *in-state only*
503-279-0100*

Pennsylvania

Keystone Peer Review Org., Inc.
777 E. Park Drive
P.O. Box 8310
Harrisburg, PA 17105-8310
1-800-322-1914 *in-state only*
717-564-8288

Rhode Island

Health Care Review, Inc.
Henry C. Hall Building
345 Blackstone Boulevard
Providence, RI 02906
New England: 1-800-221-1691
1-800-662-5028 *in-state only*
1-401-331-6661*

South Carolina

Carolina Medical Review
101 Executive Center Dr., Ste. 123
Columbia, SC 29210
1-800-922-3089 *in-state only*
803-731-8225

South Dakota

South Dakota Foundation for
Medical Care
1323 South Minnesota Ave.
Sioux Falls, SD 57105
1-800-658-2285

Tennessee

Mid-South Foundation for
Medical Care
6401 Poplar Ave. Suite 400
Memphis, TN 38119
1-800-489-4633

Texas

Texas Medical Foundation
Barton Oaks Plaza Two
Suite 200
901 Mopac Expressway S.
Austin, TX 78746
1-800-725-8315 *in-state only*
512-329-6610

Utah

Utah Peer Review Organization
675 East 2100 South
Suite 270
Salt Lake City, UT 84106-1864
1-800-274-2290

Vermont

New Hampshire Fdn. for Medical
(PRO for Vermont)
15 Old Rollinsford Road, Ste. 302
Dover, NH 03820
1-800-772-0151 *in-state only*
1-800-655-6302*

Virginia

Medical Soc. of Virginia Rev. Org.
1606 Santa Rosa Road, Ste. 200
P.O. Box K 70
Richmond, VA 23288-0070
DC, MD and VA: 1-800-545-3814
804-289-5320
in Richmond: 289-5397

Washington

PRO-West
10700 Meridian Ave., Suite 100
North Seattle, WA 98133-9075
1-800-445-6941
in Seattle: 368-8272

West Virginia

West Virginia Medical Inst., Inc.
3001 Chesterfield Place
Charleston, WV 25304
1-800-642-8686, ext. 266
in Chalestown: 346-9864

Wisconsin

Wisconsin Peer Review Org.
2909 Landmark Place
Madison, WI 53713
1-800-362-2320 *in-state only*
608-274-1940

Wyoming

Montana-Wyoming Foundation
for Medical Care
400 North Park, 2nd Fl.
Helena, MT 59601
1-800-497-8232 *in-state only*
1-406-443-4020*

American Samoa and Guam

(see Hawaii)

Puerto Rico

Puerto Rico Foundation for
Medical Care
Suite 605 Mercantile Plaza
Hato Rey, PR 00918
1-809-753-6705*
1-809-753-6708*

Virgin Islands

Virgin Islands Medical Inst., Inc.
IAD Estate Diamond Ruby
P.O. Box 1566, Christiansted
St. Croix, US, VI 00821-1566
1-809-778-6470*

Appendix D

Application for a Social Security card

Here are some examples of documents that we (the Social Security Administration) will accept as identification:

- Driver's license
- U.S. government or state employee ID card
- Your passport
- School ID card, record or report card
- Marriage or divorce record
- Health insurance card
- Clinic, doctor or hospital records
- Military records
- Court order for name change
- Adoption records
- Church or synagogue membership or confirmation record (if not used as evidence of age)
- Insurance policy

We will *not* accept a birth certificate or hospital record as proof of your identity. We will accept other documents if they have enough information to identify you. Remember, we must see original documents or copies certified by the county clerk or other official who keeps the record.

How to complete the form

Most questions on the form are self-explanatory. The questions that need explanation are discussed below. The numbers match the numbered questions on the form. If you are completing this form for someone else, please answer the questions as they apply to that person. Then, sign your own name in question 16.

1. Your card will show your full first, middle and last names unless you indicate otherwise. If you have ever used another name, show it on the third line. You can show more than one name on this line. Do not show a nickname unless you have used it for work or business purposes.

2. Show the address where you want your card mailed. If you do not usually get mail at this address, please show an "in care of address", for example, c/o John Doe, 1 Elm Street, Anytown, U.S.A. 00000.

3. If you check "other" under citizenship, please attach a statement that explains your situation and why you need a Social Security number.

4. You do not have to answer our question about race/ethnic background. We can issue you a Social Security card without this information. However, this information is important because we use it to study and report on how Social Security programs affect different people in our nation. Of course, we use it only for statistical reports and do not reveal the identities of individuals.

5. If the date of birth you show in item 6 is different from the date of birth you used on an earlier application, show the date of birth you used on the earlier application on this line.

6. If you cannot sign your name, sign with an "X" mark and have two people sign beneath your mark as witnesses.

Application for a social security card

At the end of this appendix is the form you need to apply for a Social Security card. You can also use this form to replace a lost card or to change your name on your card. This service is free. But before you go on to the form, please read through the rest of this section. We want to cover some facts you should know before you apply.

If you have never had a Social Security number

If you were born in the U.S. and have never had a Social Security number, you must complete this form and show us documents that show your age, citizenship and who you are. Usually, all we need from you are:

- Your birth certificate; *and*
- Some form of identity, such as a driver's license, school record or medical record.

We prefer to see your birth certificate, however, we will accept a hospital record of your birth made before you were 5 years old, or a religious record of your age or birth made before you were 3 months old. We must see original documents or certified copies. Uncertified photocopies are not acceptable. You may apply at any age, but if you are 18 or older when you apply for your first Social Security card, you must apply in person. Please see the special requirements if you were born outside the U.S., if you are not a U.S. citizen or if you need a card for a child.

If you need to replace your card

To replace your card, all we usually need is one type of identification and this completed form. Refer to prior page for examples of documents we will accept. If you were born outside the U.S., you must also submit proof of U.S. citizenship or lawful alien status. Examples of the documents we will accept are on the preceding page. Remember, we must see original documents or certified copies.

If you need to change your name on your card

If you already have a number, but need to change your name on our records, we need this completed form and a document that identifies you by both your old and new names. Examples include a marriage certificate, a divorce decree or a court order that changes your name. Or, we will accept two documents—one with your old name and one with your new name. If you were born outside the U.S., you must also show proof of U.S. citizenship or lawful alien status.

How to apply

First complete the form, using the enclosed instructions. Then take or mail it to the nearest Social Security office, along with the originals or certified copies of your documents. We will return your documents right away.

If you have any questions

If you have any questions about this form or about the documents you need to show us, please contact any Social Security office. A telephone call will help you make sure you have everything you need to apply for your card.

If you are a United States citizen born outside the U.S.

If you are a United States citizen who was born outside the U.S., we need to see your consular report of birth (FS-240 or FS-545), if you have one. We also need to see one form of identification.

If you do not have your consular report of birth, we will need to see your foreign birth certificate and one of the following: a U.S. Citizen ID card, U.S. passport, Certificate of Citizenship or a Certificate of Naturalization. Remember, you must show us the original documents.

If you are not a U.S. citizen

If you are not a U.S. citizen, you must show us your birth certificate or passport, and the documents given to you by the Immigration and Naturalization Service (INS). We must see original documents, not photocopies. Examples of INS documents are: Your Alien Registration receipt card (Form I-151 or I551) or Form I-94. Because these documents should not be mailed, you should apply in person.

Even though you may not be authorized to work in this country, we can issue you a Social Security card if you are here legally and need it for some other reason. Your card will be marked to show that you cannot work, and if you do, we will notify INS.

If you need a card for a child or someone else

If you apply for a card for a child or someone else, you need to show us that person's original or certified birth certificate and one more document showing the person's identity. For example, for a child we will accept a doctor or hospital bill, a school record or any similar document that shows the child's identity.

If you sign the form, we need to see your identification. Be sure to answer the questions on the application form as they apply to the person needing the card.

The Paperwork/Privacy Act and your application

The Social Security Act (sections 205[c] and 702) allows us to collect the facts we ask for on this form. We use most of these facts to assign you a Social Security number or to issue you a card; without them we cannot issue you number or card. Without a number, you could lose Social Security benefits in the future and you might not be able to get a job.

We give out the facts on this form without your consent only in certain situations that are explained in the Federal Register. For example, we must give out this information if federal law requires us to, if your Congressman or Senator needs the information to answer questions you ask them or if the Justice Department needs it to investigate and prosecute violations of the Social Security Act.

We may also use the information you give us when we match records by computer. Matching programs compare our records with those of other federal, state or local government agencies. Many agencies may use matching programs to find or prove that a person qualifies for benefits paid by the federal government. The law allows us to do this whether or not you agree to it. If you would like more facts about the Privacy Act, get in touch with any Social Security office.

We estimate that it will take you about 8 minutes to complete this form., including the time it will take to read the instructions and gather the necessary facts. If you have comments or suggestions regarding any aspect of this form, write to the Social Security Administration, ATTN: Reports Clearance Officer, 1-A-21, Operations Bldg., Baltimore, MD 21235, and to the Office of Management and Budget, Paperwork Reduction Project (0960-0066), Washington, DC 20503. Do not send completed forms or information concerning your claim to these offices.

SOCIAL SECURITY ADMINISTRATION
Application for a Social Security Card

Form Approved
OMB No. 0960-0066

INSTRUCTIONS

- Please read "How To Complete This Form" on page 2.
- Print or type using black or blue ink. DO NOT USE PENCIL.
- After you complete this form, take or mail it along with the required documents to your nearest Social Security office.
- If you are completing this form for someone else, answer the questions as they apply to that person. Then, sign your name in question 16.

1 NAME
To Be Shown On Card

▶

FIRST	FULL MIDDLE NAME	LAST

FULL NAME AT BIRTH IF OTHER THAN ABOVE

FIRST	FULL MIDDLE NAME	LAST

OTHER NAMES USED

2 MAILING ADDRESS
Do Not Abbreviate

▶

STREET ADDRESS, APT. NO., PO BOX, RURAL ROUTE NO.

CITY	STATE	ZIP CODE

3 CITIZENSHIP
(Check One)

☐ U.S. Citizen ☐ Legal Alien Allowed To Work ☐ Legal Alien Not Allowed To Work ☐ Foreign Student Allowed Restricted Employment ☐ Conditionally Legalized Alien Allowed To Work ☐ Other (See Instructions On Page 2)

4 SEX

☐ Male ☐ Female

5 RACE/ETHNIC DESCRIPTION
(Check One Only—Voluntary)

☐ Asian, Asian-American Or Pacific Islander ☐ Hispanic ☐ Black (Not Hispanic) ☐ North American Indian Or Alaskan Native ☐ White (Not Hispanic)

6 DATE OF BIRTH
MONTH DAY YEAR

7 PLACE OF BIRTH
(Do Not Abbreviate)   CITY   STATE OR FOREIGN COUNTRY   FCI

Office Use Only

8 MOTHER'S MAIDEN NAME

FIRST	FULL MIDDLE NAME	LAST NAME AT HER BIRTH

9 FATHER'S NAME

FIRST	FULL MIDDLE NAME	LAST

10 Has the person in item 1 ever received a Social Security number before?

☐ Yes (If "yes", answer questions 11-13.)   ☐ No (If "no", go on to question 14.)   ☐ Don't Know (If "don't know", go on to question 14.)

11 Enter the Social Security number previously assigned to the person listed in item 1.

☐☐☐ – ☐☐ – ☐☐☐☐

12 Enter the name shown on the most recent Social Security card issued for the person listed in item 1.

FIRST	MIDDLE	LAST

13 Enter any different date of birth if used on an earlier application for a card.

MONTH   DAY   YEAR

14 TODAY'S DATE ▶
MONTH DAY YEAR

15 DAYTIME PHONE NUMBER ▶ ( )
AREA CODE

DELIBERATELY FURNISHING (OR CAUSING TO BE FURNISHED) FALSE INFORMATION ON THIS APPLICATION IS A CRIME PUNISHABLE BY FINE OR IMPRISONMENT, OR BOTH.

16 YOUR SIGNATURE

▶

17 YOUR RELATIONSHIP TO THE PERSON IN ITEM 1 IS:

☐ Self ☐ Natural Or Adoptive Parent ☐ Legal Guardian ☐ Other (Specify)

DO NOT WRITE BELOW THIS LINE (FOR SSA USE ONLY)

NPN			DOC	NTI	CAN			ITV
PBC	EVI	EVA	EVC	PRA	NWR	DNR	UNIT	

EVIDENCE SUBMITTED

SIGNATURE AND TITLE OF EMPLOYEE(S) REVIEWING EVIDENCE AND/OR CONDUCTING INTERVIEW

DATE

DCL   DATE

Form SS-5 (9/89) 5/88 edition may be used until supply is exhausted

Appendix E

Wallet card

It is essential that your health care provider know you have executed an advance directive. Your treating physicians should be given a copy of the documents.

The wallet card is one way to do this. Fill out the card, sign and date it. Then cut it out and carry it with you at all times.

Notice to health care providers

☐ I have executed an Instruction Directive
☐ I have executed a Proxy Directive and appointed:

Agent's name_____

Agent's address_____

Phone day_____ Phone eve_____

as my agent to make health/personal care decisions for me if I am unable to do so. He/she has a copy of my complete proxy directive.

Date_____ Your printed names_____

Signatures_____

Medicare update

As this book goes to print, major changes for Medicare are imminent. The Republicans are about to unveil drastic proposals to overhaul Medicare. Although I am sure the Democrats will fight the proposed changes in their entirety, both Democrats and Republicans agree that changes need to be made for several reasons.

Based on current data, Medicare will be completely broke by the year 2003. It is a huge expenditure and budget item representing over 10 percent of all federal spending. The only items that represent a higher percentage of spending are defense, Social Security and interest on the deficit. With a major political hot-button being balancing the budget without tax increases, Medicare is one prime area to look at for cutting.

Most of the proposals to cut Medicare costs range from cutting $150 billion to $300 billion over the next few years. The annual costs for Medicare increase by roughly 10 percent per year. Proposals show capping the yearly increase to only 6.5 percent per year. This may sound good right now, but a problem will come as baby boomers start to retire and not as many people are in the work force. As a result, Medicare costs will probably rise even faster.

Few would disagree that Medicare costs are out of control and reform is necessary. But even today Medicare only pays about 45 percent of all Medicare expenses. This does not even include one of the biggest medical costs during retirement—long-term care. The vast majority of Americans will spend time in a care facility after the age of 80. (For more information on long-term care, refer to my book, *Safeguard Your Hard-Earned Savings*.) With the average costs being between $30,000 and $50,000, it is understandable how quickly people can deplete their savings.

How can we maintain a certain level of medical care without increasing our taxes, reduce costs to make this care a smaller percent of our total deficit and plan for the future as baby boomers retire? Here are a few ideas:

1. **Proactive medicine.** Medicare very rarely pays for proactive medicine. Routine physicals are not covered under the program. If preventative measures such as periodic physicals were allowed, it would save people money in the long run. For example, treating a condition such as heart disease early is often cheaper than undergoing a quadruple bypass operation.

2. **Manage Medicare costs more efficiently.** Medicare is the largest buyer of medical goods and services and, as a result, should receive the best prices. There is no question that millions of dollars are lost every year as a result of medical fraud, overpayment for goods and services and poor regulation.

   Medicare needs to spend money in order to increase regulation and reduce fraud and overpayment. There should be steep penalties and punitive damages for defrauding Medicare.

3. **Utilize managed care effectively.** More and more individuals are utilizing managed care under HMOs and Preferred Provider Organizations (PPOs) and they are very satisfied with the service they are receiving. These HMOs are private organizations and competition is fierce. In order to win your business, they need to provide more services at better prices. Since health care is a necessity, certain governmental restrictions should be placed on the HMOs.

   An excellent proposal has been introduced by the Heritage Foundation, to increase competition and guarantee quality. According to this proposal, people would receive vouchers good for the health insurance policy of their choice. When the money runs out, the individuals would be on their own. Because managed care institutions usually make money off the healthy and lose money on the sick, they have a tendency to accept the healthy. Restrictions should stipulate that they have to take anyone for the same cost. If an individual is not satisfied, he or she would have the option of transferring to another managed care outfit. Regulations could also stipulate how fast premiums could rise.

4. **Give states more control.** I firmly believe that if a state government is given a budget and required to work within it and create the best solution for themselves, through proper leadership, costs could come down. Consider, for example, Mayor Rudolph Guiliani of New York City. Since he took office the murder rate has been reduced over 18 percent in the past 18 months. He is also fighting welfare fraud. He is checking and auditing those who apply for welfare and finding many recipients have jobs in other states. This will ultimately save New York millions of dollars.

5. **Limit those who receive care.** I believe that if we pay into Medicare and Social Security, we deserve the benefits, but I also feel we need to manage costs, abuses and benefits much better. In an

effort to help the system, some individuals should opt out and be given a tax incentive. This would probably result in thousands of higher income individuals purchasing their own health insurance.

6. **Regulate charges for specific diagnosis.** As a result of medical care being a necessity, government intervention should be imposed to avoid medical profession abuses. Preferably at the state level, regulations should be imposed on what doctors can charge per diagnosis. If the doctor does not agree with the amount, he or she has the option to practice medicine in another state. This is similar to the situation in which the doctors accept Medicare Assignment, only there would be more regulation and stricter enforcement procedures.

As a private citizen, I can see that drastic changes need to be made. We can't have tax cuts equaling $250 billion (the number many Republican proposals call for) without reforming other areas. Medicare needs to be reformed by making our lawmakers more accountable for the money they already spend. Spending 10 percent of the total federal budget on Medicare is not the crime. The crime is how our lawmakers regulate the system and spend our money. Don't be a victim. Write to your lawmakers in Washington and tell them how you feel.

Index

Start educating yourself—call now!

Ken Stern is also editor-in-chief of the *Mature American* newsletter. This publication provides invaluable information for retired individuals.

The newsletter covers topics ranging from reverse mortgage, staying healthy in your older years, protecting your assets from long-term care, travel, to the best stocks and mutual funds today.

This newsletter is a must read to insure you have the facts to make informed decisions. As our way of saying thank you for investing in this text, you may request a free copy of the most recent issue of *Mature American*. Simply call 1-800-529-2884. Or, if you mention this book, you can receive one year of *Mature American* for $19.95.